Time
Will Come

A story of second chances in
life when we fall hard.

Saranya Umakanthan
Author of National Bestseller *One Day, Life Will Change*

PASSION

Published by

FiNGERPRINT! PASSION

An imprint of Prakash Books India Pvt. Ltd.

113/A, Darya Ganj, New Delhi-110 002,
Tel: (011) 2324 7062 – 65, Fax: (011) 2324 6975
Email: info@prakashbooks.com/sales@prakashbooks.com

facebook www.facebook.com/fingerprintpublishing
twitter www.twitter.com/FingerprintP
www.fingerprintpublishing.com

ISBN: 978 93 5440 070 4

Processed & printed in India

Dedication

To Lord Shiva, the Adiyogi,

My guiding light, my driving force,

My support through the darkest days of my life,

My sunshine, my rescuer to ward off the evil,

The One who will always be there for me,

My invisible thread of support to hold me strong,

My divine father, brother, friend, and

everything in this world,

I bow to you with love, devotion, and respect;

I am who I am because of you;

Om Namah Shivayah. Har Har Mahadev.

Prologue

Siddharth was leaving for his official visit to the Chennai office for a week to oversee its operations and to address his employees. All ready in his sober grey suit, he walked into the hall to see Shanaya standing on a stool. Inching upwards, she stood precariously on her toes, trying to reach the top shelf of the decorative showcase. She was dusting the awards that he had received for his entrepreneurial skills. Though that gave him a tinge of pleasure, he was angry with their maids, Aruna and Varuna, the sisters who did the cleaning and cooking for them. Though they had their own quarters, they were normally up and active around nine in the morning.

Oblivious to everything around her, Shanaya was busy dusting her husband's precious awards. She felt a surge of pride every time she touched the trophies.

Sid's thoughts lingered on his new bride. Somehow, he had pulled off the wedding ceremony without the emotional drama, and he had to admit that Shanaya had made a beautiful bride. With her exotic looks and her MBA degree, everyone had claimed that she was the perfect match for him. The job was done. He had honoured his promise to his mother.

Even without any make-up on her face, Shanaya glowed. Draped in a yellow salwar, her flower-patterned dupatta fluttered breezily, enhancing her feminine look. With her loose hair and golden ear hoops, she looked strikingly beautiful. Her healthy skin was flushed with the physical exertion. As any red-blooded male would, Sid enjoyed the beautiful vision his wife projected. She stretched again to take out the next set of trophies. His intuition forewarned him about the forthcoming fall.

"Oh God . . ." With those words, she fell.

"Watch out, Shanaya!" Sid ran towards her. With outstretched hands, he caught hold of her as she fell and they toppled together. He made sure that he took the brunt of the fall. Her body caressed him like a feather. Their eyes met. His grip tightened across her shoulders involuntarily. Her eyes widened questioningly, startled. He inhaled her fragrance, and her honey-brown eyes attracted him. He moved towards her reflexively and was lost for a moment.

"Siddharth," she stammered in embarrassment. The arch-shaped pendant in her *mangalsutra*[1] dug into his shoulders.

---

1   In the Indian subcontinent, a mangalsutra (from the Sanskrit word *mangala*, meaning 'holy, auspicious,' and *sutra*, meaning 'thread') is a necklace that the groom ties around the bride's neck in a ceremony called *MangalyaDharanam* (Sanskrit for "wearing the auspicious"), which identifies her as a married woman.

That snapped him out of the reverie. *No, I can't . . . I shouldn't*, he thought. He pushed her out of his hold vehemently.

Siddharth cursed himself. What had just happened? How did he let the situation go beyond his control? How could he have given in to this momentary temptation? And most of all, how could he do this to Mishti?

A wave of guilt overtook him. His hands went cold and clammy.

I am sorry, Mishti . . . I will not . . . I will always stay true to you. I love you.

An outsider to all his thoughts, Shanaya stood up, dusting her hands, and avoided his eyes. Sid knew that he had hurt her somehow. Going forward, he promised himself that he would not let this happen again. Her face clouded with confusion, and she was about to leave the hall when guilt prompted him to ask, "Are you all right, Shanaya?"

Perplexed, she nodded and walked away. The hall suddenly seemed empty without her presence. Siddharth dropped to his knees and covering his face with his hands, he whispered sorrowfully, "Oh God, I have created a mess!" His eyes were glazed with tears.

CHAPTER ONE

The End

Fate and fortune hardly take a microsecond to turn, and with it, life changes forever.

***

The alarm buzzed at five in the morning. Eyes half-open, Shanaya stretched her hands above her head.

"Time to get going," she instructed herself. After a quick shower, she buzzed around her new home with happiness. The early morning air invigorated her. Why had she not tried waking up early at her mom's place? She frowned. And when did her home, where she had lived for most of her twenty-three years, become her 'mom's place' all of a sudden, even in her thoughts?

She grimaced. Thinking over it for a second, she concluded that it was the side effect of her being married now.

Turning around, she observed her surroundings. This was 'her' place now—the posh penthouse with six bedrooms and an attached servants' quarter. With granite floors and delicate chandeliers, it appeared elegant, though her favourite spots were the balconies with their teak chairs, overlooking the carefully grown lush grass. The penthouse was huge for two people, and their parents seldom visited them. But she was Mrs Saxena, and she had to adapt to this wealthy lifestyle. "As if it is a chore," she chided herself with a smile.

She had moved to Bangalore after she married Siddharth Saxena—the future CEO, responsible for *India-Bliss*, the magazine. Though the market for paper magazines had fallen steeply over the years, Sid and his family had managed to hold their heads above water and retain their share of readers through the tough times. Her father-in-law monitored the North India operations and worked from their office in Delhi, while Siddharth covered the rest and operated from their headquarters in Bangalore.

As a new bride, she was determined to get that elusive title of 'best *bahu*'[2] from her extended family, which included her mother-in-law, who was staying with them for a few weeks to help her set up a new home with Siddharth. Her thoughts went to him, and she blushed. Theirs was a perfectly arranged marriage, set up by their fathers, who had been the best of buddies in the past but had lost touch over time. But ever since the two men met at Connaught

---

2   Hindi word meaning daughter-in-law.

Place, Delhi, three months earlier, there was no turning back. Their rekindled friendship pushed them to set up her wedding with Siddharth.

But no one had forced her to marry him, and the option to decide had been left to her. Shanaya first met Sid when their families got together at a restaurant in Delhi. His six-foot-tall stature attracted her. His jet-black hair along with his shrewd eyes made him droolworthy. She observed his gentleness on the surface but sensed the strength of steel underneath when he wanted things his way. With his muscular physique and his olive complexion, he was exceptionally handsome. But what pushed her to say okay to Sid, even more than his good looks, was her father's happiness. She had never seen as much unadulterated joy in her parents' eyes as when she had given a smile of approval as her response.

With her, Siddharth was friendly yet reserved. Even a week after the wedding, they had not crossed 'that' boundary. There was an invisible wall around him, which was hard for her to break through. But she was glad that he was giving her the space to adjust to her new life. She wanted to build a solid relationship with him before stepping into the intimacy of marriage. She admired him for his physical restraint.

With a smile hovering on her lips, she breezed into the hall and opened the small cabinet under the mesmerising statues. Varuna was cooking today, while Aruna was cleaning the house, and they were chit-chatting amongst themselves. She had her morning free.

Her book of mantras sat peacefully inside, taking in the positive vibes generated by the crystal arowana fish on the top. She noticed the big hardbound *Shiv Purana* underneath. The cover was blissful, and being an ardent devotee of Shiv, she was tempted to read it again. As she pulled it out, a couple of other books toppled and fell on the floor. She admonished herself for her carelessness as she bent down to pick up the books.

A red diary caught her attention. She opened the front page. SIDDHARTH SAXENA. The letters were in bold.

Could she read it? Was it not a violation of her husband's privacy? She closed it guiltily as her good intentions questioned her.

"But we are a couple," her heart argued back. Curiosity got the better of her and she opened the diary excitedly. As any eager bride would want to, she too yearned to understand her husband completely and craved for even a titbit of information about him. She flipped through the pages and found a folded piece of paper inside. Curious, she scanned through the contents. As she did so, her face turned pale. The smile vanished from her lips. Pain etched her forehead. Her world stopped spinning.

Her fingers trembled as her dreams crashed around her. She could not believe what she had just read. She closed her eyes and hoped that she had gotten the context wrong. With that fervent thought, she reread the letter once more.

"Surely it must not be. . ."

Yet the handwriting on the paper clearly indicated that it had been penned by Siddharth, even though the handwriting itself was not steady.

"How could he do this to me?" her heart whimpered.

She had been a blushing bride ten days ago, and the dark red of the peacock in her mehendi still revealed the freshness of her marriage. Droplets of tears brushed the paper. She should have suspected it, yet she had not . . . was the gala and the gaiety of the wedding just a mockery with no meaning? With all her emotional strength, she read the letter a third time as she was not able to digest the fact that Siddharth was in love with someone else . . . Mishti Hegde, to be precise.

"My dear Ma," the letter began. Shanaya continued reading with a pounding heart.

"I know that this might come as a surprise, but I don't want to live anymore. Don't cry for me, because I do not deserve your tears of love. I always wanted to be a fighter, Ma . . . but somewhere along the way I seem to have lost myself, and finding myself again seems impossible. Because life appears meaningless without Mishti Hegde. I cry with all my heart when I write her name. Yet there was a time when I wanted to live my life to the fullest, enjoy each slice it offered, and most of all, share everything with her. Yes, Ma . . . I met Mishti two years ago at our office.

I normally don't do the interviews, but fate had other plans for me. I was destined to meet her. She was one of the interns I recruited. As a part of our improvement strategy to arrest our plummeting sales, I decided to handle the recruitment myself and explore fresh talent from the market. I met her in my cabin for the first time when she came for her interview. Vibrant and vivacious, she was exactly my opposite. She was dressed brightly in a yellow kurta and salwar, and I was wearing black that day. It feels as though everything happened only yesterday . . . but I felt the instant connection even then. We interacted frequently after she joined and came to share a wonderful rapport. Her angelic looks, combined with her sharp brain, pulled me towards her. She enhanced my boring life with her lively chit-chat. She was beautiful and I believed that she was the one I was searching for.

With her magnetic eyes, she enchanted me, and I went wild over her smile. I felt energised and fervently looked forward to a glimpse of her each day. Her looks hypnotised me. But it was not just a physical attraction, for I believed that in her, I had found my other half . . . my partner with whom I could spend the rest of my life.

Together, we came up with lots of productive ideas and worked like mad. That is when the sales surged and we gained what we had lost earlier. Unsure of her feelings, I proposed to her, but she was honest, Ma. She told me outright that she loved me but warned me that things might not work out for us. Her parents were highly orthodox and they would never agree to our love. Arrogantly, I ignored what she said. I thought I could manage everything. When I think about it now, I am amazed at my confidence. I thought, what father in his right mind would say no to the future CEO of India-Bliss when he asks for his daughter's hand in marriage? Foreseeing a wonderful life with Mishti as my wife, I held hands with her. We kissed and became inseparable for two long and happiest years of my life. I showed her all the places in and around Bangalore. Like a kid, she followed me with a pulsating smile, and that gave me an urge to protect her and always keep her happy. I wanted to pamper her and put her under my umbrella of security.

Secure in our love, I thought that whatever issues arose in the future, we would kill the demons together.

When fate presented her to me, I was ecstatic, but I never knew that it could snatch her away from me as well. And when that happened, I was devastated. Like most lovers in India, it was caste that parted us. Her father did not believe in marrying into another caste. His thoughts were archaic, but Mishti accepted that. I don't blame her, Ma. She chose her father over me, and perhaps that was the right thing to do. I could see everything happening in front of my eyes, but I was powerless to stop it. I did not want to hurt her. She did not want me to get upset, but she respected her father and broke up with me. Her decision killed our relationship, but then her responsibility towards her elders was what attracted me to her in the first place. So, I can't really blame her attitude and generosity. Things moved fast, and she is now married to an NRI and is settled in London. She is miles away from me, Ma . . . and I don't even have the right to think about her. How can I think about someone else's wife? You did not raise me that way. I have my ethics, and I try to halt my uncontrollable thoughts about her, but it kills me. It brutally rips my heart apart, Ma. I thought I was strong, but this has broken me into pieces. I am shattered, and everything now looks gloomy to me. Life holds no meaning without her by my side. One more day of survival seems tough. She has taken all the colour back with her and left me with nothing. I have failed the test of life. How can I face you again?

No matter how much time passes, it can never heal this festering wound in my soul, which is growing exponentially. Why did I meet her if I am not destined to live with her? When I turn around, I see her everywhere. She floats beneath my eyelids even when I am asleep. So, how do my friends expect me to forget her and move on? It is quite impossible, and even if I do move on, it would be a dishonour to her and the memories we shared. I promised her that I could never love any one the way I loved her. All I see is an empty tunnel ahead, with blackness engulfing me. I have already messed up everything. I can't live with her memories taunting me, tantalising me, and shredding my soul into pieces. I am the unluckiest person in this world to have missed her. The future I had envisaged with her has disappeared into smoke. And without that, I don't want to stay here.

Ma and Pa, I love you both, but this will be my last goodbye. Please accept that this was never your fault. Neither was it Mishti's. I did the unforgivable, and I must pay for it. I hope that you will understand me one day and look at my grave with happiness. I am eternally indebted to you, and I am leaving my childhood memories behind for you to cherish. I don't know where death will take me, but I am all set to start the journey towards the unknown. I know this is a selfish decision, but I don't have a choice. Fate can proudly declare that it has won the war against me. I HAVE LOST!

If you are lucky enough to meet Mishti someday, please pass on the message that I wish her all the happiness in her life.

Stay blessed.

Love,
Siddharth"

Could a girl emotionally break a strong alpha male like Siddharth to pieces? Shanaya had her doubts, but the letter told her otherwise. From what she had observed so far, he was not a quitter. Had he actually gone ahead with his stupid proposal of suicide? She tensed. What had happened to him after that fiasco? More importantly, when had *she* come into the picture? If the contents of the letter were true, then she had become an intruder in her own life. She was the third person in her marriage!

"Oh God, what a mess!"

What should she do? The love-tangle between Sid, Mishti, and herself had become her marital confusion now. Dealing with this seemed like a daunting task to her. What had started as a normal day had become a life changer for her, and the worst part of it was that she did not know how to handle her husband's emotional baggage. She concluded that her life had ended even before it had begun.

CHAPTER TWO

The Painful Truth

Adversaries don't matter; it is the way you handle them
that matters. They are divine opportunities to prove your
mettle in this world.

***

Shanaya took a snapshot of the letter and then put it back inside the small cabinet. Unwittingly, she had been added to this drama, and the solution was hers to find. She did not want to talk to Siddharth over the phone about this. Drawing her breath in sharply, she went to find her mother-in-law. She had to know it all. But why had no one told her anything so far? She was stunned. Though she could count the days of her relationship with Sid, she was unable to take this issue lightly. Gloom threatened to envelop her and her vision clouded with blackness. It took her a minute or two to steady herself.

How was a newly-married wife supposed to handle her husband's ex-affair—an affair which had almost made him take his own life?

Shanaya was still trying to wrap her head around how her life had changed drastically in the past hour as she knocked at her mother-in-law's door. It was seven in the morning. As a part of her usual routine, Sid's mother emerged from her room only at eight after completing all her morning duties, which included reading the Gita. Shanaya did not have the patience to wait for her.

"Come in," Sita invited. Dressed serenely in her subdued greyish-blue cotton saree, she looked up from her book to see Shanaya walking in, looking as graceful as ever. With a perfect figure and a flawless face, she looked lovely in her white full-sleeved, embroidered kurta. But her inquisitive eyes were glazed with tears. Her fair skin was flushed too, and Sita realised that something was troubling her beautiful bahu. Observing her daughter-in-law's pale face, she asked with concern, "What is the matter, Shanaya?"

Shanaya did not want to hurt Sita Aunty by digging into this painful episode, but she had no other option.

"Aunty . . ." she stammered as she did not know where to start and struggled to find the right words.

The elderly woman lifted her eyebrows gently with all the patience in the world, waiting for her daughter-in-law to begin.

"Do you have something to share with me?" Shanaya asked, giving Sita an opportunity to reveal her son's affair.

"I don't understand, Shanaya . . ." Her mother-in-law was genuinely baffled.

The young girl let out a sigh of frustration. "Aunty, did Sid attempt suicide a couple of months ago when his affair with Mishti failed?" She cut straight to the chase.

"What?" Sita was astonished. There was an element of fear and doubt in her eyes. *Did Shanaya know?* But she tried her best to brush it away, wanting to hide the truth for the sake of her son. "What nonsense is this?" she scolded Shanaya impatiently.

"Nonsense or the truth?" Shanaya stuck to her question.

Silent, the elderly woman turned her head away.

"Don't do this, Aunty. I know you love your son. But that doesn't mean that you can destroy my life by covering up for him." Her voice was sharp.

"It is all in the past!" Sita argued.

"Is it?"

Sita Aunty reddened guiltily. With tears in her eyes, she confided in her daughter-in-law, "Don't worry, Shanaya. He never went ahead with his threat. I think he wrote that letter in desperation, having no idea whom to turn to. He did not trust anyone enough to talk about what he was going through."

Shanaya could not believe her ears. "Love makes people crazy . . . even the stronger ones," her inner voice prompted her.

"Swallowed by depression, thinking about Mishti all the time, Sid had forgotten all about his letter. He lost himself amidst the self-imposed sorrow. Fortunately for me, I found the letter and confronted him. He could not face me, Shanaya. I could read the guilt in his eyes. He told me that he could not go ahead with his decision. He accepted that he penned it because he felt lost in his life. But I could not believe that my strong boy even contemplated such a thought in his mind. How could he even think of leaving me when I have lived all my life just for him? I fainted and ended up having a heart attack."

Shanaya gasped. There was genuine pain in her mother-in-law's eyes. Shanaya felt sick for raking the old dirt up. "Aunty—" she began, only to be interrupted as Sita held up her hand, prompting her to stop.

"You deserve to know the truth, Shanaya. I should have told you even before this marriage, but I was scared that I would lose you as my daughter-in-law. I was selfish. My son needs a compassionate girl like you to be able to move on in his life."

Shanaya was not sure she needed that compliment at this point of time.

"In the end, I took a long time to recover. But my predicament made Siddharth realise that I was more important to him than his troubles and sorrows . . ."

Shanaya nodded in agreement. His mother's genuine distress had clearly pulled Sid out of his stupor.

Sita continued, "He came to meet me in the hospital . . . I could not talk to him. Though I was relieved to see him alive, his actions had hurt me a lot. I was crying . . . and on seeing my emotional plight, he broke down, Shanaya. I did not want to discuss his past. I told him that I did not give birth to him for him to throw away his life just like that."

"What was his reply?" whispered Shanaya.

"He did not answer, but his eyes revealed to me that he understood his mistake . . . he is a strong guy, Shanaya. I believe he didn't want to talk about it. My motherly instincts told me that it was momentary madness on his part. I was relieved and wanted him to move on. I refused to talk with him or to take my medicines until he gave himself a second chance. I know that I emotionally blackmailed him, but I did not feel guilty. I was doing it for my son, and he finally agreed to getting married. That is when we started to look for a suitable bride for him . . . someone who could pull him out of this rut." She looked at Shanaya's eyes with anticipation.

Shanaya shook her head in distress. "Aunty, how did you believe that he will move on and find happiness with me when he still has a huge load of emotional baggage? I was not even his choice." Her voice wobbled.

"You are his life partner . . . and you underestimate the magic of the black beads that you are wearing," Sita admonished.

When Shanaya opened her eyes wide, Sita put her hands on her daughter-in-law's shoulders and squeezed them gently.

"I know my son. He just does not realise what true love is. Had Mishti's love been true, she would never have deserted Siddharth, whatever the reason might be. I want you to teach my son all about love and life. Change is inevitable. He has to accept it and move on."

Shanaya smiled a little at her positive attitude, but deep down she knew that it was not going to be as simple as her mother-in-law said.

***

Shanaya stretched herself out on the bed as the moonbeams hit it gently. Tears rolled down her cheeks involuntarily. A cool breeze from the balcony soothed her hair, but it was not able to control the turmoil of her burning thoughts. How could her life have become so messy in just one day? She had no answers. Her thoughts voyaged in multiple directions, but the solution to her dilemma was elusive.

Earlier, she had thought that her husband was giving her the space to build a solid relationship between them, but now she understood the real reason behind his wall of reserve. They smiled, talked, and laughed, yet there was always a barrier between them . . . the invisible wall which she had failed to notice so far.

She was beginning to fall for him slowly, and she did not know how to untangle herself from this twisted emotional knot in which she was caught unwittingly. How should she even broach this subject with him? Shanaya whimpered.

She knew that he was coming back from Chennai today, yet she did not wait for him near the gate as she usually did. She winced at the thought. All these days she had been following him with her eyes like a curious puppy.

Siddharth walked into the room with anxiety. He had been quick to note that his wife had not been there to welcome him when he got back. Something was wrong. Though he knew that he could never love anyone the way he had loved Mishti, he was determined not to hurt Shanaya at any cost. He found her curled up into herself in one corner of the bed. Was she sick? He was worried. His mother had given him vague answers when he had enquired about her during dinner.

Rushing towards her, he gently put his fingers on her forehead to check her temperature. She jerked at his touch, and her eyes opened wide. He felt the wetness on her soft cheeks.

"What happened, Shanaya? Are you sick?" His voice revealed his concern.

She shook her head in denial.

"Why are you crying?" he demanded.

Wiping the corner of her eyes, she tried to smile but could not. He held her hands in support. "Tell me what is bugging you," he coaxed.

She did not respond. Seconds ticked by.

"If you believe I am interfering, I will leave," he offered.

Shanaya caught his hands, stopping him from going away. Her lips trembled as she spoke, "Siddharth . . ."

He lifted his eyebrows.

Not knowing how to begin, she asked, "How was your trip?"

He looked at her oddly. "You did not mean to ask that, right?" was his shrewd observation.

She was astonished at how her husband could read her like an open book. She would need to be more careful in the future. *He is not mine*, she corrected herself. *Never can be.*

She turned around and gave him her complete attention. She looked straight into his eyes and asked, "Who is Mishti?"

Siddharth fell silent as a multitude of emotions flitted through his heart. His handsome face flushed with guilt.

"Shanaya . . ."

"Please answer my question," she pleaded.

"Mishti is the girl I love."

His honest answer speared her heart as he spoke in the present tense, but Sid stayed oblivious of her feelings.

"So why did you marry me?"

"I . . ." He was at a loss for words because he believed that he did not have a valid answer.

Taking pity on him, she asked him gently, "Were you emotionally forced to marry me?"

When he did not reply, Shanaya got her answer. Putting her hands on his shoulders, she prompted him, "So what happens now?"

"It is in the past. I will work on our relationship," he justified himself.

"You yourself declared just seconds back that Mishti *is* the girl you love. How can you work on a relationship when your heart is elsewhere?"

"You are not planning to leave me, are you?" he asked, ignoring her blunt question.

"You are not answering me." Shanaya's frustration showed on her face. Sid did not know why he was worried that Shanaya would leave him. It was not as if he loved her.

"Oh, Lord!" she murmured as it became harder with each passing second to accept everything.

"Shanaya . . ." Sid stepped forward.

"Why did you not tell me all this before?"

"My mom chose you . . . and I promised her two things—one was my marriage, and the other was to not speak about all this to my bride before the wedding."

"Why did you not tell me after the wedding?"

"I wanted to. But each time I saw your eyes, I could not. I needed time to confess. I didn't want to see you hurt."

"I would rather listen to the harsh truth than to some lies," she condemned. His face froze like ice. He was not used to explaining his actions.

"I deserve to know the truth, Siddharth . . . and please don't tell me that you don't have to explain your past. If your past disturbs our present, then I have the right to know. If you are emotionally stuck and can't move on, then I don't think I can give you a chance to work on our marital relationship." Her voice was firm.

"Ever since our wedding, I have not spoken to her even once. We promised to delete each other's contact numbers from our mobiles once she got married. I am not in touch with her and neither is she in touch with me. The last email I sent to her was our wedding invitation with a picture of us from our engagement. What else is there to know?" He sighed in frustration and sat down on the bed.

Shanaya sat adjacent to him. "Everything," she said.

Sitting next to each other, Siddharth spoke about his past love affair—how, where, when, and what. His love for Mishti was evident on his face. Though there was no contact between them, he had neither forgotten her nor moved on with his life. It killed Shanaya to listen to all of it, but she did not show it. She kept her face blank.

"So, I am the unfortunate one who missed an angel like Mishti . . ." Sid concluded.

"She was lucky to get a guy like you in the first place," she whispered honestly.

"I am sorry that I dragged you into all this. I should have been stern with my mother and not allowed her to bulldoze me into agreeing to this marriage, but I couldn't say no to her when she was lying in the hospital bed. I did not want to hurt you, Shanaya, but I really thought that I could work on our relationship over time," he admitted. She understood how tough it was for Siddharth to even confess to everything.

Hardening her heart, she enquired huskily, "But do you want to move on?"

He thought for a while before answering her question. "Yes . . . I want to . . . but if I move on, I feel it would be a disgrace to Mishti."

"She has already gone ahead with her life, Siddharth," Shanaya was quick to point out.

"I don't think she is living a happy life," he argued.

"Are you sure?" she asked.

"She can't be happy without me . . ."

"Oh, is that so?"

"She must be thinking about me," he persisted.

She raised her eyebrows, doubting his words.

"What do you have against her?" Sid demanded.

"Absolutely nothing. But listening to your story, I don't think she loved you at all."

His face contorted with anger. "She did everything for me . . ."

"But she left you in the end, right?"

"And do you believe it is easy?"

"Why are you so blind, Siddharth?"

"Don't you dare speak a word against her," he warned.

"I am stating a fact. Mishti did not love you. Had she loved you, she would have never left you. She would have fought for your love."

"She could not go against her father. She respected him."

"Then she should have told you about it clearly in the beginning."

"Mishti told me that things would not work out between us. But I did not listen to her," he grunted.

"She told you, but then why did she encourage you anyway?" Shanaya's argument was valid.

"She could not help herself. You have never loved anyone in your life to be able to understand the emotion," he criticised.

Shanaya did not know whether to laugh or cry at that.

"Don't you think you are finding excuses on your own to justify her actions?"

"I don't have to justify her love to you. And remember, she was the one who taught me what love is."

Shanaya was exasperated. "A love that led you to destruction . . ."

Sid looked at her angrily.

Bracing herself against his fury, she continued, "Love is all about happiness . . . it is the sunshine that creates an eternal feeling that lets you grow, that lets you reach the stars and touch the skies. It is the driving force that pushes you to live each day to the fullest. But if it pushed you into darkness and gloom, then it was never love in the first place."

Sid stormed out of the room. Shanaya stared at the closed door. With all her emotions drained, she fell on the bed and punched it with her fists in frustration. She had the entire picture now. How could she even compete against his love for Mishti? The way he had defended her throughout their conversation showed where his feelings were.

Whether Mishti deserved his love or not was secondary, but Siddharth's emotions were sincere. He still lived in an illusory world with his ex-girlfriend, believing her version of love. Shanaya did not know if he was capable of loving anyone else in the future. She did not blame Mishti either, but she believed that if what she had felt for Siddharth was true, she would have fought for him. She would never have given up on their love. If she were in Mishti's shoes and was the recipient of Sid's love, she would have turned the world upside down for him.

Because her husband deserved to be loved. No one else in this world warranted it more than him at present. Let bygones be bygones . . .

Shanaya promised herself that she would show Sid that love is all about living, laughing, and growing together and what he had experienced earlier was just a mirage of love. She would make sure that he came out of this illusory mirage.

CHAPTER THREE

A Year of Chance

Friendship is the root of the tree of marriage,
and when watered with care and affection,
it bears the ultimate fruit of love.

***

Taking off her apron, Shanaya brought out the hot rotis packed in the casserole. "I will take care. I will call you if required," she reassured the maids and sent them off. The sisters left with a smile to retire to their quarter.

Shanaya set the steaming pot of vegetable curry on the dining table. Siddharth, seated at the table, observed her with interest. With absolutely no make-up, she still looked gorgeous. Feeling his eyes on her roused her interest.

"Dinner is ready . . . please call your mom," she said.

"Why don't you call her yourself?" he asked her dryly.

She let out a sigh. "You are not a helpful husband, Siddharth."

Coming out of the kitchen, she invited her mother-in-law.

"Sita Aunty . . ."

Sita walked into the dining room at her call. "Wow . . . the smell of your ghee rotis dragged me here, rather than your voice," she told her daughter-in-law delightedly.

"Who made the rotis? You? I thought Aruna made them," Sid said.

"Arre, *beta*[3] . . . I saw Shanaya making them especially for you," his mother informed him, trying to ignite the flames of romance.

"Aruna helped me," Shanaya replied modestly.

Smiling, she served the mother and son. As she was about to leave, Siddharth caught hold of her hand.

"Have dinner with us, Shanaya."

She coloured as his fingers brushed her palm.

"Yes, dear . . . please eat with us," Sita invited her gently.

To escape from his hold, Shanaya quickly occupied one of the seats in the six-seater dining table, far away from Siddharth.

"Arre . . . sit near your husband. Is he going to swallow you?" chided Sita.

"Yes, Ma . . . I am going to eat her up," Sid threatened playfully.

---

3   Hindi word for son.

Blushing at his words, Shanaya went and sat next to him. She avoided him deliberately as her feelings went wayward whenever she was close to him. But the more she tried to get away, the more interested Siddharth appeared to be.

"Concentrate on your dinner . . . don't think about him," she instructed herself. Her heart fluttered at his close proximity.

With a sensual look, Sid gently began to rub her feet with his toes under the table. She looked at him in apprehension. His featherlike caresses broke her barriers. A tingling sensation spread all over her. But his face did not reveal an ounce of emotion, and he acted all innocent.

Unaware of what was happening, Sita continued eating her dinner peacefully.

"Stop it," Shanaya hissed into Sid's ear in frustration.

"Did you say something?" Sita asked her daughter-in-law.

"Yes . . . I mean, no . . ." she blabbered.

"Ma, something has happened to our super calm Shanaya . . . look how she is all flustered," Sid complained.

"Oh . . . get lost," Shanaya murmured.

Laughing at their byplay, Sita quickly finished her dinner. "Time for me to go to bed." With those words, she washed her hands and left the dining room. Shanaya watched her mother-in-law's retreating back with apprehension.

"I know you are not cowardly enough to hide behind her," Sid commented in her ear.

Without replying to that loaded comment, she went to keep her plate in the dishwasher and washed her hands. He did the same.

"No answer?" he taunted her.

Drying her hands with a towel, she looked into his eyes, and the battle was lost. Noting the way her eyes melted, Siddharth pulled her to him. She was squashed against his hard body, and his proximity overpowered her senses. Her heartbeat became faster as he wrapped his arms around her, cocooning her in his warmth. His hand slid down her spine and rested on her hips. In return for the promised ecstasy, her hands ran through his thick hair of their own accord. His face bent down towards hers, and he took her lips in his in slow motion, taking his time to taste the honeyed sweetness of her mouth. It was addictive, and with a groan, he deepened the kiss, and she completely lost her senses.

"No . . . Siddharth . . . stop it . . ." she whispered.

He did not heed her words.

"Sid . . . please . . ." Her voice went up a notch.

Siddharth, who was passing by her room, stopped. Shanaya was mumbling something in her sleep. Ever since the grand revelation of his affair with Mishti, they had mutually agreed to sleep in adjacent rooms. With his mother leaving soon after that, it had not been a problem as there was no one to question them or the status of their relationship.

He shook her hard now, bringing her to her senses. "Shanaya . . ."

She woke up with a start; she was sweating profusely. "Are you okay?" he demanded.

"Yeah." She bent her head down as she could not meet his eyes after her hot dream.

"Did you have a bad dream?" he persisted.

"No, Siddharth . . . it was the right one," she answered him mysteriously.

He lifted his eyebrows questioningly.

"Maybe I will tell you about it someday," she promised him.

"All right . . . I am off to work," he informed her.

"Did you have your breakfast?" she asked him with concern, and then flushed guiltily since she had woken up late because an erotic dream had taken over her. To top it all, the maids were on leave today.

"Don't worry, ma'am. I had a satisfying meal of an omelette and toast," he reassured her.

Waving at her, he left.

Siddharth drove his sleek car—a BMW—out of the parking lot. His driver, Ram, a newly-married man, had gone on vacation with his wife. Sid smiled as he recalled the love he had seen on his face. His happiness had infected him.

"Maybe I will take Shanaya out for a drive," he promised himself.

The gold tint of the car shone brightly as sunlight embraced it with a kiss. Long drives rejuvenated him, but he had to delegate the daily job of driving to Ram so that he could direct his efforts completely towards improving things at the magazine, which required all his attention and time. He usually started working on his way to the office. But today, with Ram not being around, Sid was determined to enjoy his drive. He mused over the past six months since Shanaya had entered his life. He had thought that his life would end with Mishti's departure, but that had not happened.

A wave of guilt swamped him as he thought about his past. What had possessed him to contemplate taking such a drastic step? He did not even want to think about that. Had he lost his life, he would never have had a second chance. He understood that now. Life was for living. Shanaya had showed him that in a short span of time. Her energy was infectious, and he wanted to live . . . more than live . . . he wanted to laugh, dream, enjoy, and achieve. Shanaya kept telling him that his time would come.

Maybe it would. Who knew?

His mind welcomed the thought. He felt that he had been gifted with a miraculous rebirth. He was getting along well with Shanaya. Gradually, she had crept into his life as a friend . . . his best friend and confidante. Somehow, she had gained his trust. His eyes sought her out when he entered their home. He skipped going out with his friends just to taste her rotis for dinner. He knew that she cooked especially for him, even though they had maids to do the job. He loved chatting with her and discussing the day's happenings. Because Shanaya was not only lovely to look at, but she was also intellectually sharp and gave him reasonable solutions for even the most complex of issues. He loved the way her eyes lit up when he complimented her. She taught him the art of yoga, and each morning they began their day with a peaceful yoga session. Today, she had missed that session and woken up with a bad dream. Did living with him stress her out? He frowned, not liking that notion.

When did Shanaya's feelings become important to him? He was confused. Did it mean that he had forgotten Mishti?

No . . . never! he denied the idea strongly. *It will always be Mishti for me . . . Shanaya is just a friend,* he concluded. His thoughts were interrupted as he reached the office. The security guard saluted him at the gate. Waving his hand in acknowledgement, he parked his car in the basement. Holding his head high, he stepped into the ten-storey *India-Bliss* building.

***

The moment Sid left, Shanaya came to her senses. How could she betray herself to him by reacting to such a dream? She sighed in frustration. The one-year mission that she had set up for herself was not really working out. Ever since she found that fateful letter, she had promised herself that she would change things for Sid for the better. She would make him realise that life moves on with or without someone. She knew that he was a strong guy, both physically and mentally. Without that steel inside him, it would be tough to run a magazine empire all by himself. His father's contribution had gotten considerably reduced once Sid had stepped in. Mishti, however, was his Achilles heel. He might miss her, but he had to move on. Hopefully, by the end of the year, when Sid bounced back to his true form, Shanaya would leave. She could never be a substitute to Mishti all her life.

But what she did not bargain for was that while she was trying to show him the splendour of life, Sid was actually creeping into her heart slowly. His charisma and the respect he demanded wherever he went attracted her. And being a good-natured person, she knew very well that Sid would be there for her whether he loved her or not.

She did not know how she would survive without him after she left. She decided that it was better to maintain a reserved demeanour so that it would be easier for her to come out of the whole situation without any emotional entanglements. But her heart told her otherwise. Whenever she was near Siddharth, her feelings somersaulted. His accidental touch made her skin burn. She wanted to hug him every time she saw him. But her mind reminded her—*he is not yours, Shanaya. You might be married to him, but he can never be yours.*

With each passing day, she knew that she was getting captivated by him. She had to give herself space. Her thoughts were occupied by Siddharth 24/7, even her dreams were about him. Grimly, she sought a solution for her predicament. Her parents had completed their duty visits after the wedding. But she couldn't bother them with her marital woes. She had to deal with this on her own.

She missed Sid's mother, who knew her story. Had she been there, she would have definitely helped her in some way. But she had left after the first month of their marriage, saying that she wanted to give the newly-wedded couple some privacy. Shanaya racked her brain. She did not want to sit idle the whole day. Yeah, she wanted to help Siddharth, but that did not mean she had to waste her own life.

Got it . . . I have to get a job and keep my mind occupied, she instructed herself. For an MBA topper, it was not going to be a big deal to find a suitable job, and as an added advantage, she had a couple of years of work experience in marketing too. Motivated by this thought, she phoned her previous boss and found some references. Then she fixed a couple of interviews for the same day.

Feeling rather proud of herself for what she had accomplished that morning, she quickly went and got ready for the day. The doorbell rang just then. Shanaya answered it to let the maid in. Varuna looked at her in astonishment.

Wearing a grey blazer on top of a white shirt, the mistress of the house looked elegant. Her pencil skirt showed off her slim body, and the brownish lipstick enhanced her professional look.

"Wow, ma'am. You look pretty today."

"Thanks, Varuna. But does that mean that I did not look pretty before?" she laughed.

"No, ma'am! You are putting words into my mouth," Varuna stammered.

"Then?" she prompted teasingly.

"It is just that you look different . . . more like Siddharth sir." She said that as if it was a compliment.

"Okay then, wish me good luck," invited Shanaya.

The maid was further baffled.

"I will let you know why when I am back. Meanwhile, finish cleaning the house. Boil some potatoes, will you? I want to prepare aloo sabzi for Sid when I get back," she instructed her and hurried out.

She did not want to be late for her interview.

***

Siddharth let himself into the house, keying in the numbers on the lock. It was eleven thirty in the morning. One of the meetings had been postponed to the afternoon, and he was free for a couple of hours until lunch. As a norm, Shanaya sent his lunch to the office, but today he felt like sharing it with her at home. He was surprised to see that there was no sign of her anywhere in the house. Only Varuna was around.

"Varuna, where is Shanaya?" he asked her.

"She went out, sir," she answered politely.

Siddharth frowned. Normally, Shanaya did not go out anywhere without telling him.

"Did she tell you where she was going?"

"No, sir . . . she did not. She left an hour back and asked me to wish her luck. When I asked her why, she told me that she would tell me later," the maid informed Siddharth. Shaking his head, he dialled Shanaya's number. But there was no response.

Why is she not answering her mobile? Usually, she picked up his call at the first ring. *Has something happened to her? Is she in trouble?*

His brain began working overtime. Aruna joined her sister and began mopping the floor. "Did she tell you when she would be back?" Sid asked.

"No, sir . . . but she asked me to boil some potatoes. She wanted to make aloo sabzi for lunch," replied Varuna.

It was almost twelve. Shanaya still hadn't returned. He forced himself to relax. Nothing would have happened to her. But she should have told him where she was going.

Does she have any friends in Bangalore? he wondered. He felt bad because he did not even know that, whereas he was sure that she knew everything about his life.

He was frustrated. As the seconds ticked by, he was scared out of his wits. The doorbell rang just then. Halting Aruna, Siddharth rushed to open the door.

Shanaya's smile froze as her eyes met his.

"Sid . . . sorry . . . my hands are full, and I could not key in the numbers to open the lock." She gestured at her hands to show her purchases, which appeared to be clothes.

"Where did you go, Shanaya?" His tone was composed, but she could sense his anger. She rebelled at his attitude.

"Out."

The one-word answer irritated him. Here he was all worried, and she was behaving like a kid.

"I do know that."

"Can you please move aside and let me in?" she demanded as he blocked the doorway.

Sensing trouble, the sisters mumbled their goodbyes and left. Their work was done anyway.

Shanaya closed the door and turned to Siddharth. "What is your problem, Sid?"

"I was worried about you, Shanaya. I came home to have lunch with you, and when you were not here, I was scared . . ."

"Oh!" she gasped in surprise, calming down. "I did not expect you to come home for lunch or I would have informed you before I left."

She took a couple of papers out of her handbag and passed them to him.

He was shocked when he gave the papers a quick glance. It was an offer letter for her to join as a marketing executive with *Smart-words*, an online start-up magazine.

Observing his reaction, she demanded, "Are you not happy?"

"I am happy that you have the calibre to find yourself a job . . . but what was the necessity?"

"Not everything is tied to money, Siddharth," she fought back.

"I did not say that. But I thought you were happy here," he told her.

"That does not mean I have to waste my talent. I am a topper, Siddharth. I don't want to kill my professional skills." Her argument was strong.

He let out a sigh. "Okay . . . but that does not mean that you have to work for a competitor."

"*Smart-words* is just a start-up. They don't qualify as your competitor." She laughed.

"Start-up or not, I don't want my wife to work for someone else." His voice brooked no argument.

Shanaya was momentarily silenced. This was the first time that he had acknowledged her as his wife. She floated on a wave of pride, but she was not giving up her job.

"What do you suggest, Sid?"

He did not know what prompted him to say it, but he replied, "Go for an interview today at the *India-Bliss* office. We are hiring for the role of marketing executives as well."

With those words, he went out without his lunch.

CHAPTER FOUR

An Official Encounter

*When you create your opportunities, a life of adventure
awaits you, challenging you to overcome your doubts
and succeed.*

***

Shanaya walked into the reception area which
was buzzing with activity. Her wedding had been
a low-key affair and had happened in Delhi. Very
few of Siddharth's colleagues had attended the
event. She was pretty sure that with her maiden
name, no one would recognise her or place her as
Sid's new bride. So far, so good. If she got a job
here, she wanted it to be on merit and not on her
status as Mrs Saxena. She passed her résumé to
the receptionist with a winning smile.

"Ms Shanaya Dixit," the receptionist read
her name from the résumé. At her nod, she

said, "Please be seated. I will let you know when your turn comes."

This was a good opportunity for her to prove her worth, and she did not want to mess it up. It also gave her the golden chance to be with Siddharth 24/7 and do her job. Why she longed for that she had no idea. Just that her heart prompted her to stay with him.

Her name was called soon. Rubbing her hands nervously on her handkerchief to wipe the excessive sweat, she got up from the cushioned sofa. The first round of interviews was with the head of the marketing department. There were no hiccups. She cleared it in a breeze. Though she had been out of touch with the world of marketing for almost seven months, her education had never deserted her because she loved what she learnt. She had studied with her heart and never with her head. Hence, it stayed with her for life and helped her everywhere. The manager did not know that she was Siddharth's wife, and Shanaya did not enlighten him. Only two candidates out of the twenty who came for the interview were selected.

"Except for Ms Shanaya Dixit and Mr Rohit Kapoor, the rest of you can leave," the receptionist announced politely. As the crowd dispersed, she turned to them. "You will have one more interview," she informed them.

"Does it mean we are not selected yet?" demanded Rohit.

"Our chief takes the final call today . . . you can go in first. Please take the left." She showed the way to Rohit.

With determination, he walked in, and Shanaya was left to wait. Minutes ticked by. More than half an hour had passed when Rohit came out with a happy face. "He asked me to collect the offer letter from the HR department," he informed the receptionist exuberantly.

"Congratulations!" she wished him and signalled Shanaya to go in next. With a smile, she went in to meet her husband for the second time that day. She knocked on his door gently.

"Come in," he invited. The calendar told him it was the 7th of September. It was the same date as when he had interviewed Mishti three years back. Coincidence or not, here he was, interviewing Shanaya on the same day. *What is destiny playing at?* he wondered.

Without looking up at Shanaya, he glanced at her résumé in his hands. He wanted to play fair. He did not want to offer her the job just because she was his wife.

"Good afternoon, Ms Dixit," he said formally.

"Yes, Sid . . . sir." She understood his attitude and played along, always in sync with him.

"The marketing manager has given glowing feedback about you."

"Thank you, sir."

"But I do have a few questions for you before we can select you for this role," he informed her.

"I am ready for it, sir," she answered him politely.

"Ms Dixit . . . I see that you have taken a break of seven months . . . why have you taken a sudden interest in your career again?"

Shanaya let out a sigh. "Sir, I just took some time off as I got married. I always wanted to get back to work. My husband is also a busy man. With his busy schedule, I have plenty of time on my hands and I don't want to waste it. I want to do justice to my education and keep myself active."

"It sounds as if your husband is a monster," Sid remarked with a dry smile.

Shanaya laughed. "More of a workaholic," she argued.

"A workaholic with absolutely no concern for his wife . . . that is still bad," he complained.

"No, sir . . . I am proud of him and the work he does. He single-handedly runs a magazine," she retaliated. He could sense the pride in her voice and loved the way she stood up for him. Her statement about his work was the best compliment he had received in recent times.

Shanaya covertly looked at him and was surprised to see that he was observing her as well. The laughter inside her died as their eyes clashed in a magnetic duel, and the warrior in Shanaya was captivated by him. It was almost as if she was in a trance. His intense look shook her to the core. Her muddled brain refused to function under his mesmerising glance.

"Ms Dixit . . ." he called but received no response.

"Shanaya . . ." His tone went up a notch higher, and he clicked his fingers in front of her face.

That penetrated her mind. "Yes, sir!" She came back to her senses.

Get a grip on yourself, Shanaya, she instructed herself.

He changed his track. "The paperback magazine sales have dropped recently. Being a marketing executive, what do you suggest we do about it?" His query moved from personal to technical.

"Sir, I agree that the market for the magazine has gone down, but with the advent of digital books, it was expected . . . we have to change our ways as well."

"As in?" he queried, interested to know her answer. Shanaya was proving to be a worthy candidate for the job.

"We can venture into the e-market, sir . . . we can launch the digital version of the magazine, and we can run campaigns across social media, targeting the right audience."

"But there are a lot of magazines doing the same thing. That is why we have not started with it so far. How is your proposal any different from the existing ones?" he queried.

"Agreed, sir . . . there are apps providing news to our consumers, even short one-liners. I want to take that to the next step. I want those one-liners to be targeted. We have to capture the interest of the readers, apply data mining, and give them the news that they are really interested in instead of dumping generic, random stuff on them."

"Makes sense," agreed Siddharth.

His approval made her smile. It was the most beautiful smile he had ever seen, even better than Mishti's . . . his heart agreed reluctantly. He was seeing Shanaya in a completely different light today. But he could not keep comparing Shanaya with Mishti.

"I am impressed, Ms Dixit," he revealed his admiration. "Okay, let us see how well you can conclude a deal. Show me how you will tackle a problematic distribution manager to help the magazine improve its circulation," he probed her.

Shanaya stood up from her chair and requested, "If you don't mind . . ."

Then she gently dragged Siddharth out of his chair and asked him to stand in front of his table. He nodded in affirmation.

"I want to do this from the beginning." With that statement, she went out and came back in with a knock. She wanted to show her comprehensive marketing skills and prove herself before beginning her stint at this magazine house.

"Good afternoon, Mr Saxena," she wished him formally and moved close to him. That was when fate decided to turn the table on her. The heel of one of her stilettos that she had worn to the interview to create an impression broke, and to her shock, she slipped.

"Oops!" she cried.

Siddharth's mind worked agilely. Shanaya's fall would have been bad had he not moved forward to catch her.

"Thanks, but . . ." she faltered at the look in his eyes. He appeared like a man possessed by passionate desire. She could sense the battle inside him to control his wayward feelings. She watched him fail miserably on that count. His hands circled her hips. The fragrance of her shampoo tempted his nostrils. Tilting his head closer, he bent forward to sniff her hair gently. Her skin tingled as she shivered feverishly. She had not expected that her erotic dream from the morning would materialise so soon.

"Sid . . ." she whispered in a pathetic attempt to hold him off, but that backfired. Her husky voice only added fuel to the desire that burnt between them.

As if captivated by her magic, he brushed his lips across her forehead. That was when Shanaya lost herself. The candle inside her flickered radiantly and illuminated the passion surrounding them. A bolt of electricity shot through her. Sid moved his lips to her eyes as she closed them, losing her breath. She thought that he could hear her thundering heartbeat. Yet he did not stop.

Instead, he pulled her closer, and there was barely any space left between them. His adept hands released the clasp from her hair, and his fingers wove through her wavy tresses. Shanaya's legs became numb as he twisted her hair into a bunch in his fist. The sensation overwhelmed her, and she held on to him tightly for support.

"I think we have to stop," she warned him in a desperate attempt to hold on to her senses. Her words acted like a bucket of cold water poured to douse the desire that had overtaken both of them all of a sudden.

"Sorry," both of them muttered simultaneously.

"I don't want you to do this with the distribution manager," Sid joked weakly.

Redness engulfed her cheeks and her embarrassment showed.

"It was an accident," she protested.

"Yes, your fall was an accident, but what followed next was not," he persisted.

"That does not mean that I will go around romancing everyone," she denied hotly, the anger in her erupting because of Siddharth's assumptions.

He frowned, confused at her words.

"I am not like you." Her frustration showed.

The moment the words were out of her mouth, she regretted them instantly. But Siddharth caught her mistake. He moved closer to her so that she was forced to take a step back.

"What do you mean, Shanaya?" he roared. The passion in him was extinguished.

"Nothing . . ." she stammered.

"Scared to tell me?" he asked her dryly, covering his anger under a layer of sophistication.

She retaliated, unable to hold back her pent-up emotions any longer. "You kissed Mishti earlier . . . and now me. I did not mean to say that, but it just came out. I don't know what overtook me. I am sorry if I hurt you," she answered grimly with honesty.

He cleared his throat. "Enough, Shanaya . . . this should not have happened."

She was perplexed.

His frustration at his inability to control his desire became apparent. "I am sorry."

"Sorry for kissing me?" she demanded. Her eyes were glazed with tears. She was a fool for letting him break the small wall that she had built around her emotions.

Unable to reply, he redirected their conversation. "I think we have to move on instead of arguing over a worthless moment. Shall we get back to our interview, Ms Dixit?"

Shanaya fumed at this. His comment on terming their kiss 'a worthless moment' rattled her. She grabbed a notepad lying on the table and threw it at him.

It hit him squarely on his head.

"Don't you dare degrade what happened between us . . . and get lost with your interview, Mr Saxena . . . I don't care about this job." Angrily, she stormed out of his office, leaving her broken stiletto behind.

He deserved all her fury. And Siddharth knew that Shanaya was right. He just wanted to put on a show that the emotional moment did not affect him in any way. He wanted to keep a tight rein on his emotions. But with those careless words, he had tainted what had happened between them even though that was not his intention. He needed time to take this in.

Wiping his overwrought face with a handkerchief, he called his assistant through the intercom. "Please bring me some black tea, and make sure that you send the offer letter to Ms Shanaya Dixit today."

Then he sat back, a satisfied smile on his face. He was going to enjoy having Shanaya around him.

CHAPTER FIVE

A Drunken Drama

Never give up on your dreams and hopes, whatever
the reason may be; bad days are okay—letting them
overrule you is nonsense.

***

It was eleven at night. Siddharth had still not come home. Ever since she had stormed out of his office, he had neither messaged nor called her. All she had received was a call from the HR department, informing her that they had sent her an offer letter via email.

She was asked to bring a signed copy of the same and join the *India-Bliss* office the following day. She was married to the head . . . but here she was, working her way up from the bottom. To be honest, this was the way she preferred things. To her surprise, however, her reporting manager was Mr Siddharth Saxena. This put her in a dilemma.

Who had made the decision? Was it Sid? Why did she forget herself and the precarious position she was in when he came close to her? She had to be alert for both their sakes as she did not know what the future had in store for them.

But where was Sid? He was usually home by seven. She called him again. There was no response. A feeling of anxiety sneaked into her mind. Had something happened to him? She called his personal assistant.

"Hello, this is Mrs Saxena. I am not able to reach my husband. Do you know where he is?" she asked.

"Ma'am, Siddharth Sir left at seven, cancelling all his meetings after that," the assistant informed her dutifully.

Murmuring a thanks, Shanaya disconnected the call. Should she call the police? She panicked.

The doorbell rang right at that moment, cutting into her thoughts.

If it is Sid, why is he not keying in the numbers in the lock? Shanaya frowned. Something was wrong. Rushing to the entrance, she opened the door.

It was Siddharth all right, but as he stood at the door, he wobbled slightly. Shanaya rushed forward to hold him steady. "Are you okay?" she demanded.

"Shh!" he signalled with a finger on his mouth. "I am perfectly fine. Don't wake up the entire neighbourhood," he warned her, his voice rising.

His body jerked with a hiccup. From the way he smelled, Shanaya realised that he was drunk. In the six months that they had been together, she had never seen him in an inebriated state. Did the morning episode at his office push him to do it?

Hah! As if she had that power over him. Don't even think of it, she chided herself. *He could never be yours, and when the time comes when he is himself again, you will have to leave,* she warned herself sternly. *What if I lose myself here?* her pathetic heart persisted. Shaking off her thoughts, she turned her attention towards Siddharth. He was observing her with intent. Wrinkling his eyes, he came closer to her to cup her cheeks.

"What is it that is attracting me to you?" he asked her, sounding critical, as if his unwanted desire for her was a mistake.

Shanaya stood shocked at his question.

"Is it these hypnotic eyes? I could drown in the honey in them." Shanaya was stunned as he continued, "Or is it this sharp nose?" His fingers traced her sensitive skin.

"Siddharth." She badly wanted to stop him.

"Maybe it is these pomegranate-coloured lips?" he queried as his fingers brushed her lips. He stared at her, dazed. "Or is it all about you, Shanaya?"

She pulled back as if he had hit her. "What are you suggesting?"

"Did you not understand, my dear wife?" his voice insulted her.

Looking at her blank face, he continued, "I think you are trying to tempt me."

Shanaya did not know whether to laugh or cry at this complaint from her in-title-only husband.

"Why should I?" She looked squarely into his eyes.

"So that I forget Mishti!" He flashed a brilliant smile at his deduction. His words hurt her, yet she remained calm, barely showing any emotion.

"I did not tempt you. And even if that is so, what is the harm in it? You said you wanted to work on our relationship, on our marriage."

"Yes, I do, but I can never forget Mishti," he said harshly, the raw guilt evident in his voice.

Shanaya let him vent out his heart. This was a part of his healing. Seconds ticked by. He let out a sigh as he broke down a little, opening himself. He held her hands tightly. His voice cracked.

"Sorry to blame you, Shanaya. I did not mean it. You did not tempt me. And I know that I kissed you. With that kiss, I feel as if I have failed Mishti and her love."

Has he gone mad? Why is he even thinking about a girl who has already moved on in her life? It is not as if she is waiting for him. Shanaya's thoughts troubled her.

Sid condemned himself, "I have done injustice to the love I had for Mishti, and I have also destroyed your life, Shanaya, by listening to my mother. I should not have gone ahead with our wedding. I am not true to anyone."

Shanaya realised that he was hurting inside. Before he could complete his sentence, she put her hands on his lips. "Don't say that. I have never met a truer person than you."

Then, Sid dragged her to a little room, adjacent to the puja room. It was locked. She had not asked him about it so far, respecting his privacy. Now he was opening it, arousing her curiosity. It was a room full of stunning paintings— from portraits to abstracts, it had every kind of painting.

"Take a look, Shanaya," he invited.

"These are beautiful," she whispered. With an artistic eye, she observed the nuances of the artwork. She fingered each one with admiration. From paintings of peacocks to a portrait of Mishti, he had woven magic with his hands.

It destroyed her, however, to see Mishti's face. It was a huge portrait which brought out her elegance, and her haunting loveliness was projected attractively. Shanaya was disturbed to see Sid visibly upset. His forehead was beaded with sweat as he battled the old memories that haunted him.

Shanaya tried to step on neutral ground but could not. She had always had this flickering hope inside that her husband might have a change of heart someday, but the paintings seemed to convey otherwise.

Turning away from the portrait, she stopped at an abstract painting. It was elegant with bold red strokes, but something was not right. It was not like the other ones that hung proudly on the walls of the room.

"This one is bad," she told Sid openly.

"I know . . . and this is the last one I ever painted," he confided bitterly.

She was surprised.

"Why did you stop?" she asked, dreading the answer.

"When Mishti left, she took my art with her," he murmured reluctantly. There were tears in his eyes. He missed his art . . . he missed his colours . . . in short, he wanted his life back.

Hating the sympathy in her eyes, he probed, "In spite of knowing the truth, why do you stay with me? And I know that I have been a dreadful husband so far . . . no girl deserves to be caught in a life like this."

He finally asked her the question that had bugged him ever since she had known the truth about his past.

Shanaya took her stand. Time to be a little cruel. She had to make Sid understand a few home truths. "Unlike you, I take the institution of marriage seriously, Siddharth." Her voice was sharp.

Fire blazed in his eyes.

"It is not a game. If you are not ready to move on, I think you should never have married me."

"I did it for my mother, who was in the hospital . . . damn you! She did not want to recover until I said yes."

"That does not excuse you from deliberately destroying the life of an innocent girl with hopes and dreams in her eyes."

He knew that he was in the wrong here. He had scolded himself multiple times for it.

"Yes, I was wrong, and I admit it . . . but please leave if you want to. That is the best I can do to redeem myself. I don't want to hold you to this farce of a marriage. I can explain things to my mother. I should have done that much earlier. She loves you, and it will take her some time to get over it, but I will make her understand why," he volunteered reluctantly.

The conversation had become a little heated. Shanaya's eyes welled up with tears. The six months of repair work that she had done on their relationship had ended badly. Her voice wobbled as she fought back now. "Do you really want me to leave, Siddharth?"

"If that is your wish."

"Don't put this on me. I did not ask for a separation."

"I don't want to keep you in this fake relationship."

"Fake . . . don't you dare call this wedding fake!" Shanaya shot back.

Sid sighed in frustration and shook her hard. "It is not as if I want you to leave. I love having you around, but I could never be a proper husband to you . . . the husband you deserve."

"Don't act all sympathetic, my dear husband . . . you want to chase me away and mope around in the memories of Mishti."

His lips twisted in anger, and he clenched his fists.

Taking a step back, she whispered with agony, "How do I even make you understand that you are destroying yourself by clinging on to something that does not exist?"

Sid shut his eyes.

"MISHTI DOESN'T EXIST ANYMORE!" Shanaya screamed at the top of her voice, an action which revealed her anguish. She wanted him to open his eyes to the truth.

"I don't want to listen to this," he said, and was about to leave when she grabbed his hands.

"Not so soon, Sid. Running away is not going to help. I fight for what is mine. And when you said you wanted to work on our marriage, I thought you meant it," she elucidated clearly.

I fight for what is mine. M-I-N-E.

The words penetrated his mind deeply. He looked at Shanaya's determined eyes, something that he had never seen in Mishti. Could they have stayed together if she had fought for him the way Shanaya was doing? Panting hard, she looked like a lioness in action. For the first time in his life, his opinion about Mishti altered.

"How long are you going to hold on to a non-existent relationship?" Shanaya demanded.

"It exists," he persisted.

"*Existed*, but now it lives only in your mind . . . not in reality," she shoved the truth at him.

"What difference does it make?" he commented in a wry tone. His state of intoxication lessened with each passing second.

"It makes a lot of difference, Siddharth. The path you are taking right now will lead you to nothing but disaster," she pointed out in frustration.

He glared at her.

"You may be running the magazine successfully right now, but—"

He held up his hands then, signalling her to stop. The red veins in his eyes stood out as his muscles froze. Shanaya halted mid-sentence.

"Running *India-Bliss* successfully? Who told you that?"

Looking at her bewildered gaze, he laughed sarcastically. "You have no idea, right? We are a sinking ship, Shanaya."

She gasped.

"I cannot guarantee you this lifestyle for long," he warned. "You still want to stay with me? Fight for me?" he taunted.

"I have been with you for six months, Siddharth. You should know me by now . . . I am not here with you for your money!" she cried.

"Through thick and thin, you will stand by me . . . the ever-sacrificing Shanaya." Sid laughed to hide his pain. But his heart knew the truth. She would stand with him all the way, something that Mishti had not done.

"I go down and my employees go down with me. How am I going to answer to almost two thousand workers and their families? Ever since Mishti left—"

It was Shanaya's turn to stop him harshly. "No!"

He gave her an odd look. "I lost track of my professional life when she left me," he accepted guiltily, wanting Shanaya to understand him. But all he could see was her antagonism.

"We have been married for just six months, but this is not the Siddharth Saxena I know. Where has your personality gone, Sid? You don't accept failures easily, and you know it. You are the strongest person I have ever met. Your behaviour doesn't make any sense to me."

She lashed out at Siddharth, but her statements made sense to him. This was not his way of life. He knew it, and Shanaya had sensed it. He stood silent, taking whatever words she threw at him.

"Love will not let you fall, Sid. It gives you the strength to overcome your failures and the will to fight. And I believe . . ."

She halted a little and whispered, "That you never loved Mishti, Sid . . . you never loved her if you have lost yourself along the way. That is destructive."

Sid's face appeared as if it was carved from stone. He stood motionless because he believed that he deserved what was being hurled at him. Shanaya made him question if he had loved Mishti at all! And had Mishti loved him back? If so, they would have struggled together to fight for their relationship, but they had not. He began having doubts.

"When digital magazines flooded the market, you made sure that *India-Bliss* survived . . . where did that killer instinct go?"

He did not move.

"I don't see the Siddharth that your mother talks to me about so proudly in this broken version of a man before me. Had he vanished before the pre-Mishti era?"

Her words were bang on. He wanted to justify himself but he could find nothing to do it.

His eyes were brimming with emotional tears, and he was overwrought. He forced himself to get back his control.

"It is okay to cry, Sid. Men do cry." She squeezed his hands and added, "Strength is not about holding back your tears or how you handle life before you fall, but how much of your survival instincts you exhibit after you fall . . . and there is steel in you, Sid . . . you know that as well as I do. Why don't you bring that out?"

Shanaya's voice echoed around him as he was transported to another world—his pre-Mishti days. Those were the days when he had looked at fire and smiled. Those were the days when he had looked forward to facing challenges every day.

"You have lost yourself, Siddharth." Shanaya spoke what was in his mind.

Not getting a reaction from him, she got irritated. *Did she sound like an irritated wife? Was he even listening to her?*

"Sid, whatever happens, we should never give up on our life and our dreams, and you know this deep in your heart." She tapped his chest.

Silence stretched across the room. Minutes ticked by. She went closer to Sid's side, and he could sense the positive vibes she projected. He could feel her breath in his ears. Her positive energy was infectious. His muscles relaxed slowly. He felt calmer. A magical transformation traversed through him.

Standing on her toes, she pulled him a little closer and whispered, "YOUR TIME WILL COME."

The four dynamic words did the trick for him. She moved even closer and kissed his forehead, reiterating her words, "Your time will come, Sid."

A feeling of relief surged through him. A gentle breeze coming in from the balcony ruffled their faces, encouraging them to move ahead. He believed her.

Shanaya mistook his silence. Giving up, she turned away.

"I agree. I have to get myself back."

She stopped.

"I will get this magazine back on track."

She gave him a nod of encouragement

Sid noted that her lips trembled with emotion. The two of them had to start somewhere. She had tried her best to help him, and he would do the same for her.

He gave her his hand as a token of his friendship. Tentatively, she put her hand in his, glad that her words had made an impact on him.

"Friends?" he queried.

Shanaya nodded her head positively. "Go ahead, Sid. Fight it out. I will be there for you as a . . ."

He raised his eyebrows in a query.

"As a good friend." She laughed.

"Agreed." He nodded, finally ready to explore the next lane of life, leaving his guilt behind.

"I need a promise from you."

"I am not this meek always. Anyway, shoot," he answered.

"You must start painting again."

He looked at her strangely. "It is going to be tough."

"I know . . . but . . ."

"Don't you have any dreams, Shanaya?" He changed the track of the conversation.

Why was he asking this all of a sudden?

Taking in her silence, he demanded, "Your advice on dreams and hopes is only for me, it is … or is it for everyone?" His voice was laced with sarcasm.

"I do have a dream . . . I want to be a writer someday," she retaliated.

"Tell me the date," he wanted to know.

She was baffled.

"Dreams do have a deadline. Do you know that?"

His words hit her meaningfully. A flash of excitement lit up his eyes. Though his words were laced with sarcasm, she understood his intent. Supporting each other was something that worked both ways. Busy with her marital woes, Shanaya had stopped penning down her thoughts into words.

"Let the writer in you come out, Shanaya. And I promise that she will meet the painter in me for sure," he answered. Noting her grateful look, he held her face in his hands gently and looked into her eyes.

"You don't want me to give up on my dreams no matter what, and I don't want you to lose yourself within all this trauma. We all have our aspirations. I believe neither one of us should submit to whatever life throws at us in the future.

You asked for a promise, right? Why don't we promise each other that together we will reach our destinations and leave the rest to time?"

Shanaya was astonished. It seemed that the Siddharth from the pre-Mishti era was back in full force.

She put her hands into his. It was his turn to seal their deal with a kiss on her forehead.

"Count me in."

CHAPTER SIX

The Turning Point

*Joy, pain, surprise, anger, disappointment, and hope
are all wrapped into one big package for you; unwrap,
explore, and experience a roller-coaster ride of emotions to
attain self-growth, the true purpose of this birth.*

***

It was true that Shanaya's words made Sid think from a different perspective. But he had done everything for his love, for Mishti. Shanaya had implied that their love had not been strong enough to withstand all the struggles. The consequences of his actions now came to light. With a preconceived notion of love, he had let the company and his employees suffer, and they were heading towards a downfall now. Shanaya's words helped him to see that.

Love had destroyed his life. Love had hurt. And love had made him fall. It had made him do things that he would not have done under ordinary circumstances.

Yet Shanaya had argued that true love was different. She had insisted that it made one amazingly strong. Love does not let one falter in life.

"Siddharth."

He raised his head to see his personal assistant (PA). He frowned as he had not heard him knock before entering. Siddharth observed that his usually calm assistant, Prashit Diwakar, appeared flustered.

"Sorry . . . I did not knock," he stammered.

"What is the problem, Prashit?"

"I need to go to the hospital. I have given your schedule for today to Radhika. She will take care of things."

"Hospital? Why?"

"My daughter Nitika is admitted there." Prashit was on the verge of tears.

Siddharth recollected Nitika's face. He had been to her birthday party last year. Her angelic innocence had attracted him, and he had gotten along very well with the six-year-old kid. He had even promised her that he would buy her a pink teddy bear the next time he saw her.

Prashit had taken time off the previous week as well, citing personal reasons, and Sid had not delved into the matter further, giving him his personal space.

"What happened to Nitika?" Siddharth demanded now.

"She was sick and had a high fever, so we admitted her in the hospital. What we initially thought was a viral infection has turned out to be a tumour that's blocking the blood supply to her brain, and it needs to be removed immediately. Even with surgery, however, the chances of her recovery are slim." His voice wobbled with pain.

Siddharth stood up and quickly put his hands over his shoulders, but Prashit was inconsolable as he dropped down to the floor. His sobs echoed around the cabin.

"I don't know what to do. I am feeling helpless."

"If you are stressed about money, then don't worry. I will take care of everything," volunteered Siddharth. He still couldn't imagine that little girl's plight.

"I have the money, but thanks for the offer," answered Prashit dully.

Siddharth nodded. "But if you ever need any financial help, don't hesitate to ask me."

Prashit nodded. "I need some time off, Siddharth. I don't know when I can get back," he put in his request.

"I understand . . . please take care of her. She needs you."

As Prashit turned to leave, something prompted Siddharth to say, "I will come with you to the hospital."

Prashit was happy to receive the moral support Siddharth lent him. Together, they travelled in Sid's car and reached their destination quickly. Ram, Sid's driver, understood the urgency and drove as fast as he could. As they reached the destination, Prashit got down.

"Prashit, you go ahead. I will join you in a couple of minutes," Sid told him. The unhappy father went in.

After ten minutes, with a gift in his hand, Sid checked with the girl at the reception. "Nitika? Room no. 45," she replied to his query.

Thanking her, Sid went into Nitika's room, dreading what he might see. But nothing could have prepared him for the sight he encountered. He froze in his tracks. He was shocked to see a pale version of the vibrant girl he had met last year. Tears welled up in his eyes.

He saw the child's mother. She was lost in her own world, barely noticing him when he entered the room. There was no sign of Prashit anywhere.

Nitika's head was wrapped in a big bandage. She was hooked to an IV drip. She recognised him the moment her eyes met his.

"Nitika."

"Boss Uncle!" That was her nickname for him.

Touching her fingers tenderly, he nodded. Her voice jolted her mother's attention.

"You are Prashit's boss, right? I am sorry, sir," she apologised.

"That is okay, ma'am. Please call me Siddharth."

Before their conversation could continue, Nitika interrupted, "Is that mine?" She had noticed the gift in his hands. He brought his attention back to the girl.

"Yes, my dear. Delivered as promised." He passed the teddy bear to her.

Unwrapping it with Sid's help, Nitika exclaimed, "Wow, it is pink! You remembered!"

"I did remember, Nitika . . . how could I forget my promise to you?"

"But you never came to see me after my birthday," she complained.

"True. I was busy, but I have come now; are you not happy?"

She shook her head. "I like you, Uncle, and I want to see you now and then . . . not just once," she informed him fervently.

"We can meet frequently. What is stopping us?" Siddharth winked, touched by her friendliness.

"This," she replied, and pointed to the bandage on her forehead as she tugged at his sleeve to pull him closer. Siddharth's heart went out to her.

"I am not sure, Uncle. I heard the doctor speaking to my dad. I don't have many days left to live. Even if we plan to meet, we can't," she whispered. "I want to live, Uncle. I want to live for many days. Not just for some time as the doctor said. I want to enjoy life with my mom and dad. I want to travel to a lot of places. I want to bathe in different rivers and enjoy the sea. I hope I can get enough time for that. I love the water, Uncle."

In that moment, Sid realised how precious life was. And how cheaply he had tried to throw it away without caring for anyone around him. Looking at the crying mother, he realised how his own mother would have felt if he had gone through with his suicide mission.

This little girl was fighting for her life, whereas he had given up on his. His lips trembled in sadness. Words failed him. Tears rolled down his face as he stood there in a state of utter hopelessness. He noticed that Nitika's mother just stood by listlessly, unable to bear her pain. He struggled to swallow the ball of sorrow that threatened to choke him. *Stay strong, Siddharth. Get a grip on yourself,* he told himself. He teased Nitika, taking away the heaviness of the situation.

"Did you know that eavesdroppers never hear good things about themselves?"

"I did not eavesdrop, Uncle . . . they thought I was sleeping, but I was not," the child replied seriously.

Prashit joined them then with a bunch of medicines.

"Hmm . . . so, Nitika, you have a desire to live a long life, and you love water?"

She agreed with a tender smile.

"In that case, how about we make a deal?"

"Deal?" she queried as her eyes opened wide, projecting innocence.

"Yes, Nitika; in business, we make deals. I will make one with you. You have to believe that you have a long life ahead of you."

"What will happen if I believe that?"

"If you believe that, then you will live long. Fight your pain, Niti. Don't worry. Soon your pain will run away, frightened of you. You can then play in the water. Your time will come." He whispered the last line in her ears.

Looking at her incredulity, he continued, "If you do so, I will take you to the beach in Chennai."

"Really, Uncle?" She was all excited.

"I promise, Nitika."

Waving at her grateful parents and a smiling Nitika, Siddharth left the room and waited at the hospital entrance for Ram to bring the car around.

His advice to the kid was spot on. But why did he not follow it himself?

Easier to preach than practice, he criticised himself.

There are people in this world who long for additional

days in their life. But he had thoughtlessly contemplated suicide. He should have either fought for Mishti or accepted the defeat gracefully. Nobody had the right to even think about throwing away the gift of life. He sighed.

Shanaya's words were one hundred per cent right. He had known all this earlier, but his heart had refused to acknowledge it. But that was going to change from now on. He would fight back . . . fight for the sake of his company and his employees. Most of all, he had to fight against all odds to regain his old self.

The moment he reached his office, he took out his iPhone and called his mom. At the third ring, she answered the call, "Beta, how are you?"

"I am fine, Ma," he replied. But a sense of uneasiness enveloped him. Seconds of silence ticked by.

"What happened, Sid?" Sita asked anxiously, frightened by his silence.

"Nothing. I called you to say I am sorry."

Sita was taken back. Never had her son apologised to her in recent years. In fact, she had scolded him multiple times for his arrogance.

"Sid, is that really you talking?"

"Ma!" he silenced her with the agony that was evident in his voice.

"I am confused, beta. What are you apologising for?"

"I . . ."

Understanding the seriousness of the situation, she remained silent. She was astonished to hear her son, who was otherwise bold enough to speak about anything, struggle for words.

"I am extremely sorry that I even contemplated giving up my life . . . I am sorry that I did not value what I had . . . and I am sorry that I decided to quit. Instead of facing the truth, I took the easy way out. And most of all, I am sorry that I made you unhappy and sick."

His eyes glistened with tears.

Waves of his sorrow and genuine regret reached Sita.

"That is okay, beta. As long as you understand your mistakes, no harm is done," she consoled him.

"Are you happy, Ma?"

"I will be happy only if you lead a happy life with Shanaya," she replied honestly. Ever since she had brought Shanaya into their home, Sita had been feeling guilty for disturbing the life of an innocent girl. She wanted Siddharth's reassurance.

There was a knock on his cabin door just then.

"Ma, I have to go. Someone is here," he told her.

Frustrated that she had not gotten a reply, Sita gave up and ended the call.

It took Sid a few seconds to control his emotions and get a grip on himself.

"Come in," he invited.

Shanaya walked in holding a couple of files.

"I am done with all the joining formalities, sir. I was asked to meet my reporting manager," she told him formally.

"Is something wrong?" she enquired as she noticed his reddened face.

"No . . . give me those files, and please call me Siddharth . . . that's what my employees call me," he ordered brusquely.

Nodding, she handed over the files to him.

"My PA's daughter is in the hospital, so you will be playing the dual role of a marketing executive and my PA till Prashit is back. Your cubicle is just outside my cabin, and you will report to me directly."

The facility team had given her the cubicle close to his. Coincidence or not, it was the same seat where Mishti had sat earlier. He had asked the HR department to ensure that Shanaya reported directly to him. She was a junior employee, and the HR team was surprised at his request, though no one dared to question him. He did not want his wife to report to someone else. He frowned at his thoughts.

Since when had he started considering Shanaya his wife?

He turned to her. "The HR team reported that you were late to work today," he criticised.

"My cab was late." Her voice was stoic.

Her lips trembled with anger at his query. She dug her fingers into her palm in an attempt to control her anger. To Sid, she looked absolutely cute. Her simple white kurta and her black leggings enhanced her figure. Wearing her hair up in a ponytail and with hoops in her ears, she looked elegant. Her angry stance added to her attraction. For the first time, he admired her without any guilt.

Shanaya blushed at his blatant appraisal of her.

"That is not a valid excuse," he aroused her anger by a notch.

"People with BMWs can't understand how much time an office cab takes to reach its destination, managing all the potholes in the roads."

He twisted his lips. "I do understand, Shanaya. But why would you take the office transport? I believe you are married . . . why don't you ask your husband to drop you to work?"

She had not anticipated this interrogation. Was he ready to take her to the office every day? But she caught his mood. It bordered on playfulness, and she felt her stress draining away gradually.

"Yes, I am married, Mr Saxena . . . and my husband is a very busy man. He can't drop me to work."

"Did you even try asking him, Ms Dixit?" he argued.

"No, I did not, because my husband is a big shot, Mr Saxena. I don't want my colleagues to know that I have a CEO for a husband. I don't want to get any preferential treatment in the office, which I am sure I will get if someone saw me with him intimately."

The moment she uttered the word 'intimately', she covered her mouth as if she wanted to swallow the word back.

"I . . ." she stammered.

"So, if you consider a car ride with your husband an intimate gesture, how would you categorise a kiss between you guys?"

She appeared flustered at his question. Her reaction made him hot. He started to enjoy having her around him at the office.

"I think you are crossing your limits, Mr Saxena. That is a private question which I will answer only in front of my husband."

"Hmm . . . point noted, Shanaya."

What had happened to Sid? She had a feeling that she was speaking to a completely transformed person. It would be hard to hold her heart against him now.

"What is the point of all this, sir? Going forward, I promise I will not be late to office," she stressed.

Noting that he was not convinced, she blurted out, "If you are not reassured, I promise to ask my husband for a lift as you suggested, and I will make sure that no one sees us."

"Good move, Shanaya . . . welcome to *India-Bliss*."

He shook hands with her. Her soft hand felt like velvet against his. Raising it up, he kissed her fingers deliberately.

She stood astounded.

"Good luck, Ms Dixit," he whispered.

CHAPTER SEVEN

My Partner

True love inspires you to grow. It is neither selfish nor self-seeking. With trust and hope as the supportive pillars, love heals you.

***

A month had passed since Shanaya joined *India-Bliss*, and Siddharth had to admit that she excelled in all her tasks. Right from handling his meetings in Prashit's absence to her suggestions about marketing the magazine better, she did a fabulous job. Little guidance was required from his end. To be honest, he loved having her as his assistant, and she was proving to be a valuable addition to the marketing team. Slowly, she grew on him without him being aware of it. She became an integral part of his life.

Shanaya had left earlier than usual from the office today. She had other issues to sort, besides finalising the plan for bringing *India-Bliss* back to the top.

It was 11:35 pm when Sid reached home. The moon hid behind the gloomy clouds, and it was dark except for the flickering streetlights. Parking his car, he rang the doorbell. He did that purposely, instead of opening the door himself. He loved to see Shanaya opening the door for him with a welcoming smile. However, there was no response.

Had Shanaya already gone to bed? Had he disturbed her beauty sleep? He felt a little guilty. Normally, she waited up for him no matter how late he was.

Unlocking the door, he let himself in. Taking off his shoes, he tiptoed into the hall, making sure that she did not wake up at the noise. He saw that his dinner—rotis and aloo sabzi—was still hot, as it had been packed neatly in casseroles. He had eaten a sandwich for dinner at the cafeteria, and unwilling to waste the food, he put it inside the fridge. He chided himself for not messaging Shanaya that he might be late.

Ever since his big secret had come out, they had stopped the pretence of sleeping in the same room. Her room was adjacent to his, and he had this innate desire now to see her sleeping before he went to bed. Anxious, he tried the doorknob, and to his surprise, the door was open.

He was astonished to see her asleep at her study table, half sprawled over her open laptop. The screen revealed that she was preparing the plot for her book. He smiled. She had taken his advice. He minimised the Word doc, and found that there was one more window open, which revealed a picture of him. She had marked parts of his face— 'black eyes', 'wavy hair', 'stern look', 'sculpted nose'.

Was she picturing him as the hero or the villain of her story? Shrugging off his doubts, he called out her name. But she slept on innocently, like a baby. A smile was plastered on her face.

Who is she dreaming about? Definitely not me. Sid frowned as he did not like the path that his thoughts were taking.

Gently, he lifted her from the chair. Murmuring incoherently, she snuggled into his chest. She held his shoulders tightly, as if holding a pillow. Her lips brushed his arms, and she felt all satiny in her pyjamas. With her face devoid of all emotions except for a lopsided smile, she still managed to look adorable. And he wanted to hold her like that for the rest of his life. The thought jolted him.

He carried her to the bed and bent down to lower her safely into it. But she tightened her grip, not letting him go. The gesture appeared childish, but somewhere he sensed the little girl hidden within her, and it touched him more than he wanted it to. He noticed an old teddy bear tucked behind her pillow. The moment he pressed its soft fur into her hands, she let go of him and held on to the toy as if it was her lifeline. Covering her with the quilt, he drank in the sight of her. He realised that he was getting addicted to her and did not want to think about Mishti anymore. It gave him a feeling of relief. Bending down, he gave her a gentle kiss on her forehead. Then, switching off the lights, he walked away reluctantly.

***

Though he was exhausted from the hectic day at work, Siddharth struggled to sleep. The soft foam bed was no comfort that day. His window was wide open, letting the moonbeams inside. The clouds had vanished. The night view was enchanting, yet it disturbed him in a strange way. He missed Shanaya. How was that even possible when he had literally spent his entire day with her? It didn't seem enough. Sleep eluded him. There was a crucial meeting with an interested investor tomorrow. What was wrong with him? It was not as if he loved Shanaya. With a frustrated sigh, he threw off his quilt. His thoughts were chaotic. He could not put a name to the feeling that was haunting him at this odd hour. He had to vent his emotions.

A spark of inspiration hit his brain and he decided to follow it through. It had been a long time. But the question was—could he do it? Was it even possible? Doubting his own ability, he opened the door that led to his private domain.

His forehead was laced with sweat. His paintings seemed to mock him. The colourful lines and strokes disturbed him mentally. Mishti appeared to smile sarcastically at him from the big canvas on which he had painted her portrait.

"Don't you even try, Siddharth. You know that you can't do it without me," her voice teased him out of nowhere. Closing his ears, he willed the voice to go away.

"Go away, Mishti," he whispered. "You are not a part of my life anymore, and I will do what I want to," he warned her gruffly.

But he heard the sound of her tinkling laughter inside his head.

"Get lost," he shouted. He went forward, grabbed her painting, and threw it on the ground with a thud. The frame splintered into pieces.

In her bedroom, Shanaya jerked awake at the sound and ran towards the room. She found him sitting with his head bent, hitting the granite floor with his fist.

"Sid!"

His eyes met hers, and she noticed the tautness in his face. He was sweating profusely and his eyes were dazed. She bent down to retrieve Mishti's portrait. Inching quickly towards her, he held her wrists tightly to stop her from picking up the painting. "Leave it there," he told her brusquely, lest the glass pieces hurt her hands.

She appeared wounded by his words. Dropping the painting, she put her hands on his shoulders. "I want to paint, but I don't want her to disturb me," he whispered. The thought that Mishti was still able to distract him in this manner distressed Shanaya. His pain induced her pain.

"She never disturbed you, Sid; you made your own disturbances."

"I know. That is why I broke it."

Her eyes sought the broken painting. "Doesn't matter if you love someone or not. You should never give them the key to your happiness."

"I agree, Shanaya. I have always lived my life by my rules . . . my way . . . but I don't know what happened when Mishti entered my life. I have let her rule all my emotions, thoughts, and actions. And I deeply regret it. I don't want to do it anymore."

"Prove it," Shanaya invited.

Taking the painting out of its shattered glass frame, he broke it into two and threw the pieces into the dustbin. Empty silence filled the space. His heart thudded at his action. Even Shanaya was shaken.

"That is not what I meant. Neither breaking the picture of your ex nor burning her photo is going to help you. The change has to come from within," said Shanaya.

He lifted his eyebrows as if questioning her.

Before she could elaborate, he changed track. "Did I disturb your sleep?"

"No," she denied. She was truly shaken by the sound of the painting getting torn apart and by his hoarse voice.

That is when a strange thought occurred to her. "Who put me to bed?" she asked with embarrassment. The agony of the earlier moments was broken.

"Who else is here?" he retorted.

She blushed at his answer. "I do have the right, you know," he stressed as the redness in her cheeks invaded her face. His mood turned topsy-turvy in a matter of seconds, and that was the magic of Shanaya. What seemed like a life-sucking depression did not look like that anymore. Suddenly, none of it mattered to him in any way.

The clock struck twelve. Shanaya brought out an empty canvas and fixed it on the easel.

"When I said 'prove it', I meant this." She opened the paintbox, which had an array of colours inside. He looked at them with an ache in his heart.

"Go ahead, Sid . . . I believe this is why you came here in the first place. No better time to start than now."

His reluctance showed on his face.

"What is stopping you, Sid?" she demanded. But he stood in silence. Taking the brush, she forced it into his hands. Gently, she pushed him a little, coaxing him to move closer to the canvas. His face was pale as a sheet, and he stared at the canvas as if he was looking at a ghost. But his mind demanded that he fight his demons once and for all.

"Go ahead," she whispered again. Her voice pulled him out of the trance into which he had fallen unknowingly.

"I will," he promised her.

His instincts pushed his fingers to put some paint on the canvas. The moment the brush touched the canvas, he stopped. His emotions went haywire. He struggled to contain them and closed his eyes. "I am trying, but I can't," he muttered wearily.

She put her hands on his hands. "You can, Sid, and you know it," she reiterated softly.

Their fingers were entwined. Her hold gave him his confidence back. She nodded reassuringly. Holding her gaze, he began painting. The strokes danced on the canvas in a perfect blend of colours. Shanaya admired the way his hands moved deftly on the canvas. Once he began, he was so engrossed that he became completely oblivious to everything around him. She settled down on a sofa to watch him. Half an hour passed by.

A beautiful red rose emerged on the canvas.

"See, I told you." She stood up with a smile, admiring the end result. It was stunning. The dewdrops on the flower looked real. She gave him an exuberant hug with an exhilaration that entranced him. His trial of overcoming the past was over.

"The artist is back, Sid," she told him firmly, with a happy sigh.

"YES."

He knew that, and his eyes revealed his excitement because he felt that words were not enough to tell her what he was going through at that moment.

***

Shanaya was still sleeping as Siddharth got ready in his usual office suit. His grey blazer fit him snugly over his white shirt and accentuated his taut muscles. Usually, Shanaya was ready by this time and they drove to the office together. She had been reluctant to join him initially, but he had managed to convince her. He did not want her to get sandwiched between the men in public buses and office cabs. He had requested Ram to pick her up on the days he had to leave early. But she always preferred travelling back in a bus and God only knew why. She told him not to bother Ram multiple times a day, and he had argued vehemently that it was his job. Her security was his concern. That was the best he could do for his friend.

Is she just a friend? his heart asked him bluntly. He did not have an answer.

But she was going to be late for work today. He did not feel like waking her up after the previous night's drama. *Let her rest.* With that thought, he left her to sleep in peace.

Since Akshaya was around to help him out today, Siddharth did not look out for Shanaya until lunch. Akshaya was a woman in her forties, and she filled in as his personal assistant when Shanaya was not there.

"Let us take a break, Akshaya," Siddharth told her. It was almost one o'clock. They were preparing for a meeting with an influential investor—Adhik Khanna—today. If everything went well, Adhik's cooperation could help them generate more funds for the company.

"Have you brought your lunch, Siddharth?" Akshaya asked him.

He shook his head to indicate he hadn't.

Was Shanaya in yet? He frowned. Then he checked his phone for messages.

Reached office.

Her crisp message had come at eleven in the morning, which he had missed.

"Why don't you try our cafeteria lunch today? If the CEO eats there, many employees might be tempted to have food there. We can generate more funds for the upcoming project then," Akshaya remarked jokingly.

"Ha ha! I don't need a reason to have food in my own company cafeteria. I do get my sandwiches from there quite often. But it has been a long time since I had lunch at the cafeteria. Come, let us go," he replied, laughing.

Taking the elevator to the top floor, they reached the dining area.

Ordering two aloo parathas, Siddharth aimlessly scanned the crowd in the cafeteria to pass the time as he waited for the food to get ready. Akshaya was busy attending a call from home.

Sitting two tables away was Shanaya, and she was not alone. Siddharth stared intently at them. Talking animatedly to the new recruit, she did not notice him at all.

An irrational feeling of anger gripped him. His softness subsided as his manly instincts took over. In all these months, she had never interacted with him in that way. Her eyes sparkled and her face portrayed enthusiasm.

He tried to recollect the newcomer's name.

"Hah . . . Rohit . . . got it," he muttered.

"Did you say something, Siddharth?" Akshaya turned to ask him.

Shaking his head, he signalled her to continue with her conversation. His eyes involuntarily travelled towards Shanaya. Wearing a pink saree, she looked exceptionally pretty. Her thick hair was plaited with a bow, and she wore pearl studs in her ears. Her mangalsutra was tucked inside her blouse. He cursed himself. It was his idea that no one should even doubt that Shanaya was his wife. She had to climb to the top through her own merits and skills.

He noticed that Shanaya and Rohit were sitting close, with their heads almost touching. Holding her hand with his, Rohit was talking now, and he patted her shoulder with his other hand. She reacted with a pout, and they laughed together. Their cosy conversation disturbed him more than he could have imagined.

No . . . don't do this, Shanaya.

His rational brain told him clearly that it was just an innocent meal with a colleague in a crowded cafeteria.

Maybe they are sharing official information as they joined the company on the same day.

But the green monster of envy triggered a wave of possessiveness in him. It refused to listen to his brain.

Taking his plate of aloo parathas from the counter, he went to join her. "Hello, Shanaya . . . Rohit."

"Good afternoon, Mr Saxena," stammered Rohit. Even Shanaya was shocked to see him at the cafeteria at this time. She had woken up late and had not had time to prepare his lunch today. Guilt overtook her. Even though Sid kept telling her that she need not pack lunch for him every day because they had maids to do it, she loved cooking for her husband, and she knew in her heart that Sid loved her cooking. But today he had also asked the maid to not prepare lunch for him. So, she had assumed that he was going out for lunch. She had not expected him to have lunch here.

Sid acknowledged them both as he pulled up a chair to sit at their table. Rohit was stunned to see Siddharth joining them. Siddharth then turned to Shanaya. "I did not see you at your desk today. Were you late?" His anger took a different direction.

"Yes, Siddharth . . . I was tired."

"I don't see any tiredness now," he remarked as he recalled the way she had been conversing with Rohit.

Shanaya felt as if she had been caught red-handed while stealing candies from a jar. Guilt swept over her. She understood that he was not happy about something, but was not able to pinpoint what it was. He was acting like a bear with a sore head. He should have woken her up if he had needed her.

"Was there any issue in the morning?" she demanded as anger took over her.

"I took Akshaya's help today," he retorted. After finishing the call, Akshaya came to him.

"Siddharth, my kid is sick. He needs my attention. I have to leave. So, I have cancelled my lunch. Am sorry . . . I can't be around today." She sounded rueful.

"That is okay, Akshaya . . . Shanaya is back. She will help me out, if she is not too busy chatting here with Rohit that is," he answered sarcastically.

The trio gasped. Shanaya looked mortified. Rohit sat uncomfortably, perched on the edge of his chair. Akshaya had been with the company for almost five years now. Not once had she noticed Siddharth sounding petty. What had happened to him? At times, he did mentor junior resources, but he had never treated them this way.

"It is my lunchtime, Mr Saxena. I don't chat around during my office hours," Shanaya retorted.

Seeing the heat waves erupting, Akshaya took her leave. Rohit got up. He did not want to fight with the boss. "I am almost done, Shanaya. I will catch up with you once you are done with your work." He waved as he left.

CHAPTER EIGHT

You Are Mine

Be the best friend to your life partner. Be the one whom they can dream with, eat with, live with, and share all their nonsensical chit-chats with.

***

The moment Rohit left the table, Shanaya turned to Siddharth with anger blazing in her eyes. But he was eating his aloo paratha with apparent calm.

"What is the problem, Siddharth?"

"Chill, Shanaya. Everyone is watching," he responded dryly.

"That did not matter to you a few seconds back," she retorted.

"Right . . . what others think does not matter to me."

They were going around in circles, and she still did not understand his issue.

"Anyway, what was your interesting conversation with Rohit about?" He shot the loaded question at her casually, appearing to be uninterested.

"Why should that matter to you?"

"Curiosity, lady," he drawled.

"And curiosity killed the cat," she argued.

"And I am alive, waiting for your answer."

Shanaya couldn't believe that he was seriously asking her such a question.

"Is it a rule at *India-Bliss* that all the employees must reveal their private lunchtime chats to their boss?"

"Not everyone . . . but you have to." His voice was firm.

"Which century are you living in?"

He shrugged his shoulders. "I am the boss here." The term 'private conversation' rattled his brain.

On the other end, Shanaya fumed.

How dare he? All these days, he tortured me repeatedly by talking about Mishti . . . but all of a sudden, he is playing the role of a possessive husband, and that too because of a simple conversation with a friend. How crazy could he get?

She had to draw the line firmly here.

"I will not answer to you about my private life, Mr Saxena." Her eyes raged.

Siddharth neither backed down nor batted an eyelid.

"You can't sideline me, Shanaya. If Siddharth Saxena, the CEO of *India-Bliss*, isn't going to get an answer from you, then it is Siddharth Saxena, the husband of Shanaya Dixit, who is asking the same question."

She was dumbstruck at the way he put the query right back at her feet. "I don't have a husband here."

"Don't play with fire. I can prove otherwise."

"A husband is not someone who just ties the mangalsutra. He is more than that. And the magic word here is 'love' . . . and I am answerable only to a real husband who loves me with all his heart, not to a namesake husband," she taunted.

The moment the words were out of her mouth, Shanaya realised her mistake. But words once spoken cannot be taken back. Sid lost his pallor.

"I am sorry, Sid. I don't know what got into me. I did not mean it that way."

He sat frozen, not saying a word. Seconds ticked by.

Shanaya was close to tears. Taking his plate of half-eaten parathas, he got up from the chair. "You are right. I should never have asked you. I don't have any right over you as a husband. Even I am perplexed over why I reacted this way."

She suggested, "Maybe you were jealous . . ."

Siddharth laughed harshly. "Jealous? I don't think so. Possessiveness belongs in a relationship of love, something which is not present anywhere in the picture in our relationship. What we share is a good relationship, a friendship. Don't confuse yourself."

It was her turn to go cold.

"Have you lost your capability to deal with love because of your past?"

He left the table without an answer. Her question burnt him. Shanaya let the teardrop trail down her cheek, not really bothering that a couple of people at the other table were watching her.

Back at her desk, she doubled her pace of work. It kept her mind off her complicated husband. She was busy sending out an email to a writer when Rohit came to her desk.

"Hey, sorry that I left midway."

"That is okay, Rohit. It did not matter," she responded with a smile so as to not hurt him. He was a good friend of hers and she did not want to burden their friendship with small hiccups like these. Anyway, it was not his problem to deal with.

"Is the boss always such an ogre?" he asked.

Shanaya laughed at his words. "I don't think so."

"But you are the lucky one, you know . . . you report to the great CEO himself," he goaded.

"It has its merits and drawbacks."

"Hmm . . . but why do I get a feeling that there is something more turbulent hidden behind the calm exterior that you project?" His curiosity was triggered.

"Maybe your instincts are wrong," she misguided him.

"Or maybe you both are in love!"

"No way. Anyway, he is married. Don't you know?"

"I am your friend, Shanaya . . . my ears are always ready to listen to whatever it is that troubles you," he told her.

"Thanks," she murmured. She needed someone to lean on.

"But I do need something in return." He grinned.

She thumped his hands. "For a moment there, I actually fell for your friendly act."

"Arre, Shanaya, I am looking to rent out a small apartment. My parents are moving to Bangalore to stay with me. I have shortlisted a few places. But I need your help in choosing the right one and in setting things up."

She affirmed, "Deal. We will do it tomorrow."

***

That evening, Shanaya left the office before Sid without waiting for him. She had to calm her raging mind. When she had come to know about his big secret, all she had promised herself was a year of giving a chance to their relationship for it to grow into something meaningful and to bring Siddharth out of the rut he was stuck in. Months had passed, and she believed that she was the one who was falling into this pit of love, though she had denied it vehemently when Rohit had suggested it.

Of course, Sid was getting back in form. He fine-tuned his ideas and came up with new plans and campaigns for the magazine. But in terms of their personal relationship, he was the same. He called her his friend, but to her, he was becoming more than that. As far as he was concerned, it appeared that he had set his boundaries clearly. He was not going to fall into that trap again and he probably still loved Mishti, even though he was not moping around anymore. But how could she be sure?

It would be better to be on guard when he was around, because she knew that the pain of unrequited love was unbearable. But recently, his attitude towards her had changed. If she labelled him as 'friend', he behaved more like a husband. And if she labelled him as 'boss', he occupied her mind and soul the entire day.

He had told her that the last conversation he had had with Mishti was when he had sent their wedding invitation to her. She believed him.

Did he even realise that he was being given an invisible hand of support? She thumped her hands on the sofa. She was probably never destined to be loved.

Don't fall for him, Shanaya, she told herself.

Her mobile vibrated on the side table. Wiping her tears, she answered the call. Unbeknown to her, Siddharth walked into the apartment just then and listened to her one-sided conversation.

"Hello, Ma," she answered.

Siddharth had seen her mother at their wedding and once again when she had visited their apartment soon after. He had suspected that Shanaya did not share a good rapport with her parents. Her interactions were minimal with them during their visit. Though he had noticed this, he had not asked her about it, not wanting to hurt her further. Hence, he was pleasantly surprised and happy to see her mother calling her. He could see a little smile tugging at the corners of Shanaya's lips.

"Yeah . . . yeah, I am so happy, Ma."

"He treats me well."

"Siddharth is the best husband anyone could ask for."

"And he loves me a lot."

"Yes, Ma . . . I love him too."

She hung up her mobile. Her words were like a slap on his face. By covering up for him, she had proved her mettle as a faithful wife. He felt like a scumbag for spoiling her future. She deserved better than him. The truth hit him coldly. His dinner was ready on the table but he did not feel like eating. Changing into his pyjamas, he went to his room.

Shanaya whimpered as she listened to the slamming of the door. Done with the call, she stared at the closed door of Sid's room bleakly. What had she done to deserve this?

He had not spoken a word to her since the afternoon fiasco. Their usual friendliness was disturbed. She had her self-respect as well. Locking herself in her room, she vented out her frustration on her laptop's keyboard. Letters transformed into words . . . and words transformed into emotions . . . and emotions translated into a beautiful story!

The next day, she woke up when her mobile vibrated with a message at seven in the morning:

```
Good morning, sleepyhead. Remember your
promise to help me? I am ready. We will
start out at eight as planned. Meet me
in front of the city park. I will pick
you up from there.
```

"Oh dear." Shanaya cursed herself. She had completely forgotten that she had promised to help Rohit with his house-hunting. Rushing out of bed, she asked Aruna to prepare sandwiches for breakfast. Varuna was cleaning the house. Sid was out jogging. She had a quick shower and dressed casually in a pair of blue jeans and a yellow T-shirt. Tying her hair into a ponytail, she beautified her eyes with soft strokes of the eyeliner and added a dash of pink to her lips. She was all set for the day.

Siddharth walked into the house to see his wife all dressed up, and frowned. Normally, she slept late on Saturdays, recuperating her strength for the upcoming week.

Good that she is finding ways to engage herself, he thought.

Towelling his hair dry, he broke the ice. "Going out?"

Shanaya smiled as he dropped his ego. She responded enthusiastically. "Yes, Sid. I am doing some house-hunting today."

"House-hunting? Why would you do that? We have a palatial apartment here."

"Ha ha, true. This is not for us, though. I am house-hunting for my friend," she told him.

"Friend?" He sounded mildly curious.

"Yeah . . . pampered by his parents, Rohit is not self-sufficient enough to do this alone. He needs help," she replied.

Siddharth stopped in his tracks. What did she even think she was doing?

"Rohit? The guy from the cafeteria?"

She stopped as she caught the undercurrent in his tone.

"Yes, the same guy. Rohit is my friend. And I will definitely help my friends. That is my nature, and anyway, I am not doing it for free. He has promised me a bike ride as a token of our friendship . . . I can't wait. It has been a long time since I went on a bike ride," she conveyed her stand clearly.

He would do anything to stop this stupid outing now. Her innocence showed, and he wanted to be at the receiving end of that.

"I understand your friendship, Shanaya, but what about work?"

"On a Saturday?" she retorted.

He twisted his lips. "Don't you want *India-Bliss* to survive?"

She blinked at his query.

"I am meeting the head of *ITSectYouth* today. We will be discussing how to enhance our digital edition. *ITSectYouth* is run completely by young people, and that is what this magazine wants—inputs on digitalisation as well as on the taste of the youth."

His idea made a lot of sense and could indeed be a turning point for the magazine. Seeing the wheels turning in her brain, he pushed ahead, "I would have taken Prashit if he had been here . . . but you are filling in for him, right?"

He tied her up, not physically but with his words.

"Yeah . . ." she said reluctantly, not able to find even one reason to deny his request.

"Please give me five minutes to get ready. And I am glad that you wore casuals today. We are meeting young prodigies."

Not even waiting for her answer, Siddharth rushed inside his room. Sighing, Shanaya flopped on to the sofa. She would have to convince Rohit to push their plan to some other day. It would have to wait. She had to do this for the magazine's sake.

Sid whistled happily in the shower. He had known that she would resist him, but after living with her for all these months now, he understood how to tackle that resistance. With a smile on his lips, he dressed in his favourite combination, a white T-shirt and black jeans. With a couple of sprays of perfume and an expensive brown leather watch on his wrist, he was ready to spend the day with Shanaya—outside their home and beyond the walls of the office.

His perfume taunted her nostrils as he joined her in the living room. Shanaya caught her breath.

But, boy, was he handsome!

He looked all macho in his attire and portrayed a ruggedness which attracted her. How was she going to stay cool for a complete day without falling for his lethal charms? *Extra red alert!* She panicked at that thought.

He clicked his fingers before her. "Shanaya, are you there?"

"Yes." She flushed with embarrassment as he told her that he had called her thrice to bring her back to this world.

"Let's go," she told him.

Deciding on informal shoes, they locked the house knowing that the day was going to be eventful both personally as well as professionally. Excitement coursed through them. Taking a call on his phone, Sid walked ahead into the parking lot.

Shanaya stood outside on the road, waiting for Ram to bring the car out. Their driver was always a call away since he stayed close to their apartment. Siddharth would have informed him already to pick them up.

The persistent honking of a bike's horn disturbed her, and she frowned. The biker, wearing his helmet, stood close to her, as if he wanted her to join him. The predominantly black colour with orange-tinted lines, gave the bike a solid look.

She scowled, showing her displeasure, but he did not move.

"Are you mad?"

He did not respond. Angrily, she moved ahead a few steps, but the biker followed her and stopped exactly where she was.

"Get lost! I will call the security. My husband will be here any moment now," she threatened.

Though the biker had a good physique, he would be no match for Sid. "My Sid is a strong guy . . . you will never be able to beat him. Run off before he comes," she warned him.

"Call your 'Sid' then," a familiar voice challenged her as the biker took off his helmet.

"Siddharth," she stammered.

"So, you agree that I am your he-man who'll come to your rescue?"

She was embarrassed. "Do you own a bike? I never knew."

"You never asked."

"Where was it parked?"

"At the other end of the parking lot. We do own the bike parking slots over there."

She pouted. "Whatever . . . are you good at riding this monster?"

A dig at him! Siddharth retorted, "Come, let me show you how good I am."

CHAPTER NINE

The Growing Bond

When life suffocates you with problems that overwhelm you, deactivate your panic mode. Detach yourself and cut out the invisible chord of emotions. The solutions are right in front of you.

***

Shanaya got onto the bike behind Sid, legs on either side of the back seat. They took off and the bike jolted and gained speed as it cruised through the main roads of Bangalore. She felt as if she was slicing through the air. The cold wind brushed her face vigorously. The ride invigorated them, and their issues evaporated into thin air.

"Hold on tight," he warned, noting that she held the side grip loosely; he was concerned about her safety. He halted abruptly as a two-wheeler came towards them from the wrong side of the road.

Shanaya toppled forward onto Siddharth's back. He smelled of mint and sweat. She could feel his warmth, and her skin tingled all over.

"Are you all right?" he demanded. Her soft fall on his muscular back impacted him more than he wanted to admit. He wanted to bring her to his side, hold her close, and hug her tight. His heart demanded that he make her stay this way all his life. He shrugged off his unwanted thoughts. He did not want his life to get entangled in emotional knots anymore.

"Yeah . . . nothing to worry." Her words cooled his ardour a little.

He stopped at a secluded corner, away from the traffic. "Better hold me like this." With those words, he pulled both her hands, so that they could hold his hips.

"Now I'll know that you are safe," he added.

For Shanaya, it was an act of blissful torture. Sid did not have an extra ounce of fat on his body. She felt that Siddharth was overstepping the limits of their friendship. She was not used to roaming around on bikes with men, holding them this close. The rides with her friends were just a means to reach the destination, but this was something different . . . something else. Her body shivered in spite of his warmth.

She loved the feel of his body against hers. It became difficult to hold on to her senses when he taunted her nostrils with the smell of his aftershave which wafted towards her despite them wearing helmets. Her instincts prompted her to move closer to him. Unconsciously, she hugged him. She needed him . . . his support.

Siddharth was out on his bike after a long time. Her gentle hug made him mad. Her head was nestled against his shoulders. He leaned back, and there was hardly an inch between them. He wanted to stop his bike and kiss her right there in the middle of the road. Controlling his excitement, he increased the speed. The cool wind and the pleasant atmosphere made the ride absolutely exhilarating.

"I have never felt like this, Sid," she whispered into his ears.

He turned a little towards her, keeping his eyes on the road. "I know." Their helmets touched, and he could feel her tremble despite the barrier.

"Are you cold?" he asked her.

"No," she whispered.

"Oh God . . . Shanaya," he growled. "What are you doing to me?"

She asked herself the same question. What had possessed her to get so close to Siddharth?

Before she could answer him, they reached *ITSectYouth*. It was an old but decent building which had been modified into an office. Stopping the bike, Sid had to be still for a few seconds to get back his breath and poise. The ride with Shanaya had heightened his senses. They got off, and he sought her eyes, trying to find an answer for her behaviour. She lowered her head, evading the silent query.

"This does not end here, Shanaya . . . but we don't have time to talk about it now," he warned. She was not able to meet his eyes.

Siddharth shook hands with the CEO of *ITSectYouth*.

"Mr Rahul Khanna."

"Call me Rahul . . . and I hope you don't mind if I call you Siddharth," he informed him.

The moment Rahul noticed Shanaya, his face lit up.

"Hey, Shanaya, what a surprise!"

He came forward and hugged her. Shanaya acknowledged him happily. Noting that Sid had stiffened beside her, she turned to him. "Siddharth, Rahul was my batchmate from the IT department back in college."

"Rahul, Siddharth is my boss. I work for him," she said.

The official relationship that Shanaya tried hard to portray to others was irritating Sid. He glared at her but let that pass by.

"Wow, new job . . . new life, and I heard you got married as well. Who is the lucky guy?" Rahul queried.

"Yes, I am married. You might know him now . . ." Shanaya's reply was evasive.

"And you did not invite me to your wedding," Rahul criticised her in mock anger.

"I did invite you. You have to check your mail once in a while," she retaliated.

"Oh. I would have seen it, but no guy wants to see the wedding invitation of the most beautiful girl in the college," he stated matter-of-factly.

Embarrassed, she turned away. "Still so modest, Shanaya. You know that almost all the guys in the college pined for one smile from you, but no one could compete with Mayank. Are you still in touch with him?"

She willed him to stop. Rahul did not know that Siddharth was her husband. "No."

"You made a striking couple," he remarked.

"That is enough, Rahul. I am married now. Talking about the past is inappropriate," she told him.

"Come on. You act scared, almost as if your husband is here," he taunted.

"Oh, shut up." Shanaya stopped his tirade further. Her cheeks were red with mortification.

Mayank? Who is he? She has not mentioned his name even once to me. An emotion he could not name burnt Siddharth. Realising that he could not fish out anything from Rahul, at least not for now, Siddharth steered the conversation back to official mode with a smile, controlling all his annoyance. "So, shall we begin?"

"Sure, Siddharth . . . let me call my team. It is almost lunchtime. You can tell us your requirements over lunch. Join us."

Three more youngsters joined their conversation. The meeting went on for a few hours, but it was effective. "That is our requirement . . . we have already digitalised the magazine, but we need that special something—an X factor to take it forward and help it stay alive in this competitive environment," Sid summarised.

"Understood, Siddharth. We always do our best at *ITSectYouth*, but for our friend's boss, we'll do a lot more than that," Rahul laughingly remarked.

"Can we get an initial report by next week?"

"Yes, sure," affirmed Rahul.

***

Siddharth itched to know about Mayank. But how could he ask Shanaya directly? They did not share that kind of a relationship. He observed her in his rear-view mirror. She had lost her earlier enthusiasm and was silent. Her hands held his shoulders lightly, but she was lost in her own world.

"Shanaya," he called.

The bike spluttered right at that moment, and he was forced to stop it at the corner. "Damn . . . what happened?" he cursed. He pressed the self-starter button, but the bike refused to start. He tried once more, but nothing happened.

"Double damn," he muttered.

"Relax, Sid . . . let us take it to a mechanic," she advised.

"I do know what to do, my dear friend." His voice was laced with sarcasm. They could see the evening sun peeping out partly from behind the clouds.

She bristled at his reply. Observing her reaction, he added, "I feel bad about making you walk, Shanaya."

"I am not made of clay," she chided him. Taking off their helmets, they placed them across the handlebar so that they could move comfortably.

He pushed the bike, and Shanaya walked along with him. It allowed them to get a glimpse of the food stalls along the street.

The aroma of food invited them. She tugged at his shirt wistfully. "Oh God! Looks yum. So tempting, Sid. Shall we try that chocolate sandwich?"

Siddharth would have said yes to anything she asked for now. The pleading look in her dewy eyes captivated him. Mishti was not even in his thoughts. Mayank was forgotten temporarily.

"I have a sweet tooth," she persisted.

Siddharth saw the child in her. "Why not?" He grinned at her eagerness.

"*Bhaiya*[4], two chocolate sandwiches," she ordered. Turning towards Sid, she said, "My treat."

He laughed in agreement. Parking the bike nearby, he joined her.

"I have not eaten in these roadside shops for years," he confided.

"Tsk!" She twitched her nose. "You have missed a lot in your life. You can find the tastiest food here—even better than the five-star hotels."

"Ahh, the food guru speaks," commented Siddharth dryly.

"I do have a food blog, sir . . . and I have reviewed all the roadside savouries you get in Delhi," she retaliated with pride. With each passing second, he was finding out something new about her.

"You never told me about this blog." He frowned.

"You never asked me, boss."

He let out a deep sigh. She pulled him close to the shop.

"Look how wonderfully he makes it," she appreciated the shopkeeper, who was busy making the sandwiches.

With butter smeared on either side of the bread, the man was loading bits of shredded chocolate on top of it. Sid smiled at her admiration. Her happiness rubbed off on him. He felt completely relaxed after a long time.

---

4   A Hindi word, which means big brother. It is also used as a polite and
    respectful form of addressing a man, especially one older in age.

"Looks tasty," he remarked as the microwave melted the chocolate on the sandwich. The shopkeeper passed a plate to them. Shanaya's eyes revealed her love for food.

"The first one is for you," Sid invited.

She did not care about who was watching her. Her attention was riveted on the sandwich. She took the plate from him.

With her eyes closed, she tasted it, forgetting herself.

"Delicious," she commented after a couple of bites.

Siddharth watched her longingly. Her cheek was smeared with a brown dash of sweetness, and the melted chocolate dripped from the corner of her mouth. The vision she presented would have tested the virtue of a saint. The drop of chocolate was about to drip down, and he was sorely tempted to taste it from her soft lips before it was wasted on the ground. He swallowed his yearning with difficulty. His gaze fell on her throat, as she relished her bite. With glaring clarity, he understood that he wanted her. He craved for her. He moved close to wipe the traces of chocolate from her velvet-soft cheeks. She opened her eyes, and they were caught in a sweet chocolatey spell that enchanted them. His fingers stopped at her lips. Her eyelids fluttered. Their mutual attraction tugged them towards each other, breaking the wall of the barriers they had built around themselves.

Shanaya opened her eyes wider, and reality slipped farther. Their eyes met and kept them spellbound. The minimal crowd, the flavour of the food, and the enticing fragrance of the brown bars added to their romance. He wanted to put his hands around her shoulders. Heart-pounding excitement swept through her as she anticipated his next move.

The shopkeeper called them. "Sir."

They shook their heads, clearing their muddled thoughts.

"Arre, what is it, bhaiya?" Sid turned to him; his frustration was evident on his face.

"Your sandwich . . ." he said hesitatingly, understanding that he had disturbed something important between them.

Shanaya's senses returned to normalcy. It was a public place, for God's sake!

Getting his plate with the sandwich, Siddharth proceeded to enjoy it. "I love this." He licked his fingers, enjoying the taste. His genuine enjoyment melted her.

"Don't do this, Sid," she wanted to warn him, just to safeguard her heart. Because she knew that she was falling for him—lock, stock, and barrel.

Noting that the shopkeeper had started watching them with curiosity, they moved away after finishing the delicacy.

Pushing the bike, they walked again, enjoying their togetherness amidst the silence. The street was empty.

Plop! The raindrops hit the ground.

Wordlessly, they turned to look up at the sky which had darkened noticeably. The rain hit them forcefully.

"What a day! Run . . . let us go." With those words, Sid dragged his bike and ran to stand underneath the thatched roof of a closed shop nearby.

He did not notice that Shanaya had not joined him. After parking the bike safely, he turned to look at her. She was still standing at the exact spot where he had left her.

"Shanaya, what are you doing? Come here. You are getting wet," the authoritative tone of the husband came out.

What if she gets sick? She looks like a young kitten.

"No, Sid, please . . . let me stay. This day could not have gotten any better," she cajoled him.

"You are getting wet, Shanaya," he warned her.

"So what?" Her defiance was evident.

Shaking his head, he went to drag her back into the safety of the shed. She resisted him as he pulled her. The raindrops hit them vigorously, drenching their clothes as they filtered down through the yellow flowers and leaves of a big tree nearby.

"Poor flowers . . . look at them . . . they are getting wet," she informed him sulkily. Noting the look in her eyes, he stopped. "They love the rain. No point in worrying about them," he said, explaining things to her as if she was a little girl.

"So do I," she told him stubbornly and shook off his hands. She trapped him with his own words.

The blue sky had vanished, and black foamy clouds took over. The rain intensified, sweeping the earth with vigour.

"Shanaya, it is pouring," he complained as cold rainwater ran through his shirt.

"Hmm . . . but it smells wonderful, Sid . . . the smell of the mud, the trees, flowers. It is absolutely magical." Her voice squeaked with excitement.

She swirled around naughtily. Her T-shirt fluttered with her movements. Siddharth had never seen this wild side of Shanaya.

"If you ever want me to forgive your mistakes, all you have to do is apologise right under the rain, amidst the woods, with the flowers over me. I can exonerate you from the biggest of your sins." She sounded as if she was drunk.

"What do you mean?" he demanded seriously.

Shanaya giggled naughtily. Observing the mischievous look in her eyes, he sighed. "You are testing my patience, Shan; have you gone mad?" Sid demanded.

She stuck out her tongue in response. She turned to him, moving closer. Pouting, she claimed, "You are a spoilsport, boss."

"Enough, Shanaya."

Bending a little, he dragged her into his arms and lifted her.

She squealed in surprise. "Sid! Everyone is watching us!" she muttered to hide her awkwardness. She could feel the fire in his touch consuming her, in spite of the cold rain.

"That did not stop you from dancing like crazy!" He laughed and added, "But who is everyone?"

She turned around and looked at the road. It was empty. The one or two people she had seen earlier had fled when the rain had started. Her cheeks blushed crimson. Carrying her safely to the bike, he dropped her back on the ground.

"Be a good girl," he advised as he bent a little and rummaged through the front pouch attached to his bike.

"Got it." He took out the ever-useful item that he always carried with him—his blue towel. His eyes sought Shanaya. Leaning towards the edge of the shed, she was still trying to capture the raindrops, smiling.

Losing his patience, he pulled her towards him and commented, "If you insist on behaving like a little girl, I have no choice but to show you that you are a woman."

She understood his intentions as his fingers caressed her face gently. She could feel his hot breath against her face. His perfume, potently mixed with the smell of rain and mud, made her dizzy. She pushed back a wet lock of hair from his forehead, a gesture which ignited him. Electricity whizzed around them, binding them as his fingers moved from her cheeks to her lips. Her hands wound around his shoulders of their own accord and ran through his wet hair. His hands spanned her waist as his lips touched hers. She closed her eyes to enjoy the heady sensation that he was arousing within her.

A car passed by them just then, splitting the air with a loud honk of its horn.

The sound brought them back to reality with a jerk, and they moved away from each other guiltily, even though they savoured the passion that they had stolen from each other.

CHAPTER TEN

The Trust Factor

Trust is so delicate and fragile an emotion.
When it shatters, its broken shards pierce the heart
and murder the soul.

***

The new week began with a touch of the sun's warm golden sheen. Siddharth wanted to begin a new life with Shanaya. He was sure about that. Mishti's memories did not disturb him anymore, and he was ready to take their relationship to the next level, but he had to solve the mystery of Mayank. Did he still mean a lot to her? Was that why she had never spoken about him? His thoughts threatened to overrule him.

Sakshi walked into his cabin. She was the new recruit who had been hired the day before as part of the sales team. Her performance in the interview had been incredible, but what really caught his attention was the little detail in her résumé—she was from the same college, department, and batch as Shanaya. Yet he did not remember seeing her at their wedding. Had his wife invited all her classmates? He was not sure.

"Hello, Sakshi."

"Good morning, sir."

"Please be seated," he invited her.

Sakshi appeared worried. Why had she been summoned to the CEO's room on her first day?

"Make yourself comfortable, Sakshi. I am not an ogre who is going to throw you out of your job on the first day. Your performance was great in the interview."

"Thank you, sir." She relaxed a bit but still did not understand why she was here.

"Do you know Shanaya?" He cut to the chase.

"Shanaya . . ." she strained to remember.

"Your classmate," he prompted.

"Yes, sir. How could I ever forget her!"

He lifted his eyebrows in a query.

"She was my best friend."

"Was?" he questioned.

Maybe that is why she did not attend our wedding.

"Shanaya was my best friend. But why do you want to know about her?"

"She is close to me," he admitted.

"I don't talk to her anymore." Sakshi's hatred was evident.

Taking in that fact, he dug for more information. "Why?"

"She took Mayank away from me."

He gasped. The Shanaya he knew would never do something like that. "You probably misunderstood."

"Hah, so you are one more guy caught in her trap," she remarked.

He could sense a layer of jealousy in her tone.

"Relax, Sakshi. It will help me sort out my life if you can share the details of what happened with me, but if you don't want to and feel it is too personal, I will not pressurise you. You can go back to your desk."

Sakshi did not mind. It was just a small piece of information requested by the great CEO himself, and she was a little desperate for this job, which paid her well.

"All right, I will tell you what happened. But if she is close to you, why don't you ask her yourself?"

He had asked himself the same question. He was curious to know about Mayank and the part he had played in her life, but guilt stopped him from asking her. It wasn't as if he had a clean slate himself, what with the baggage of Mishti that he was carrying. They did not share an open relationship either, where the partners could ask each other anything.

"She is close . . . but not that close," he replied truthfully to Sakshi.

"Whatever." She shrugged and began telling him what she knew about Shanaya. After all, it was the boss's request.

"I believe you are talking about Shanaya Dixit, right? But she was Shanaya Das once upon a time," she told him mysteriously.

Sid was shocked as he listened to Sakshi narrating the story. She took him through Shanaya's childhood, and the scenes unfolded right before him, where he was able to visualise her dimpled face and her innocent eyes.

***

Place: Delhi

Time: Twenty years ago

The four-year-old Shanaya waved to Mr Das, her father.

"Look how beautiful my angel is," he commented.

Mrs Das stared proudly at the pretty picture her daughter portrayed. In her white frilly frock, she looked cute. The dimples in her cheeks stood out against her clear, fair skin. Her hair was tied into two ponytails on either side of her head with pink satin ribbons.

"Papa, where are you going?" Shanaya frowned when she saw Mr Das taking the cloth bag that he normally took with him when he went out to buy groceries.

"I have to get some dal for your mom. She has promised to make my favourite dal *khichdi*[5] today."

"I'll come with you, Papa."

"No, darling; it is late. You stay at home."

"But Papa, if you don't take me with you, you have to get me some ChocoHearts," she demanded.

"ChocoHearts?" He frowned. He had no idea what that was.

Mrs Das volunteered the information. "Shanaya has become addicted to ChocoHearts, dear. They are heart-

---

5   Khichdi or khichri is a popular dish in South Asian cuisine made of rice and lentils.

shaped candies with melted white chocolate in the centre and are wrapped in different coloured sheets. And each time I cross the corner shop, she pesters me to buy some for her."

"Anything for my maharani, even if she demands the moon," Mr Das answered his little daughter with a grin.

"I don't want the moon, Papa . . . just the ChocoHearts," she reiterated childishly.

He smiled. "Okay, I will bring you what you asked for. But what will you get for me in return?"

She thought about it seriously for a couple of seconds.

"I will make you coconut laddus, Papa. I know how much you love them. Ma, you will help me, right?"

Her mother nodded. With the deal sealed, Mr Das waved at his daughter and left. Laughing, she ran into the kitchen to prepare what she had promised. With a smile on her lips, Mrs Das joined her.

Together they made the coconut laddus with love, and Shanaya waited for her father to return with her ChocoHearts, but instead, they were disturbed by the shrill ringing of the landline telephone.

"Hello," her mother attended the call.

Mrs Das' smile vanished slowly as she stood frozen like a statue. Though she could not understand what had happened, Shanaya sensed that something was wrong.

"Ma." She tugged at her saree.

Her mother did not reply. Tears rolled down her cheeks, and she whispered, "Shanaya . . . Papa will not bring you ChocoHearts anymore."

"I have the laddus ready for him, Ma. Will he at least come back to eat them?"

Her mother shook her head.

"But Ma, he promised me," she wailed.

Shanaya could not comprehend why her father was brought back in a stretcher after that. She did not ask her mother because she was crying badly. Her neighbours and relatives joined them. She sat silently with them. Near and dear ones assembled at her home and kept murmuring repeatedly, "Heart attack at such a young age . . ."

Not really understanding that her father was dead, Shanaya went to her mother. "Ma, I don't want the ChocoHearts. Please ask Papa to get up and play with me . . . and eat the coconut laddus I made for him," she told her innocently.

Her mother hugged her tightly and cried again.

It took Shanaya more than a year to understand that Mr Das was no more. She missed him like hell.

***

A year had passed since Shanaya met Mr Shikhar. He was her new father. Shanaya knew that Mr Shikhar had no money. They moved into his house, which was tiny and not painted. She was now seven years old. Initially, she had not wanted to talk to him. She understood that even her mother did not like him that much. Only as she grew older did she realise that the pressure of being a single mother had forced her mother into accepting Shikhar as her husband. And they never talked about ChocoHearts in their home again.

They sold their old house. Shanaya could not understand why Mr Shikhar took all the money. When her mother removed all the pictures of Mr Das from their old house before moving, she had begged her mother for one picture of him.

"Keep it, *beti*[6], but don't show it to Shikhar. I am doing it for you. I understand that no one can replace your father, but you have to put in some effort. Shikhar is trying his best to be friendly with you, and you should do the same."

Shanaya's conversations were stilted with Mr Shikhar, and she remembered her mother's advice. She tried her best, but she could not imagine anyone else as her father. She could not speak properly with her mother either. Mr Shikhar was always watching them like a hawk.

One day, after she got back from school, she went to her room. There were two rooms in the house, one for her and the other for her mother and Mr Shikhar. She opened her old trunk to retrieve the picture of her father.

"I did it, Papa. I won the medal in the race today!" she exclaimed.

Her usual monologue continued.

"There were seven participants from different schools, and I beat them all. Are you happy, Papa? Ma will be happy too. I will show this to her after Mr Shikhar goes out tomorrow."

She bent forward and kissed the picture.

---

6   Hindi word for daughter.

"I love you, Papa, but I am still angry with you. You broke your promise . . . you never got me my ChocoHearts and never came to eat my laddus either."

The door creaked just then. She turned to see Mr Shikhar standing at the doorway. She fumbled to put the picture back into the trunk.

"I never knew that you are good at sports," he said, forcing affection into his voice. She looked at him with fear.

"Don't be afraid, beti. I was giving you time to adjust to your new home."

She stayed still.

"Congratulations, Shanaya," he wished. She did not reply. Her heart still pounded at this unexpected encounter with her stepfather.

"I am proud of you." He put his hand on hers.

With doubts flooding her mind, she put her hand into his tentatively. "That's my girl," he said and gave her a bear hug.

"Will you call me papa?"

She nodded. Hearing their conversation from where she stood hidden behind the door, her mother went to the kitchen happily. This was what she wanted. Her daughter needed that male support, the guiding force.

"Pappaa," little Shanaya stammered.

Shikhar laughed. "You will get used to it. Don't worry."

The child smiled timidly.

"I heard what you were saying. Do you like ChocoHearts very much?"

She nodded. "I do, but—"

"I promise you that I will get you some."

She looked at him in bewilderment.

"Come along with me; let me buy you some ChocoHearts. I don't make promises that I can't keep."

Shanaya nodded as she joined him. Her heart fluttered with happiness. Maybe her mother was right. Mr Shikhar liked her enough to buy her ChocoHearts.

Her mother waved at them as they left the house. They walked to the shop hand in hand. Her friend Tanya stopped them on the way. "Is this your new father?" she asked.

"Yes," Shanaya informed her proudly.

"Where are you going?"

"He is buying me ChocoHearts," Shanaya replied happily.

"Lucky you. Bring some to school tomorrow."

Tanya waved at Shanaya. She walked away with Mr Shikhar.

Noting that Mr Shikhar was taking the wrong route, she told him, "Papa, the ChocoHearts are available in the shop in the other street, not here."

"You are little, Shanaya. You don't know a lot of things. You have to leave certain things to the elders to sort them out. They sell bigger ChocoHearts in the shop I am taking you to."

She was satisfied with his answer and walked silently with him. Mr Shikhar's pace picked up.

"Papa, you are walking too fast."

"Learn to walk fast then," he replied curtly.

Bewildered, the little one whispered, "It is so dark here."

"Don't pester me, Shanaya."

"I am scared, Pa . . . Papa," she stammered.

"Scared? Don't be."

Darkness overtook the sky, and the eeriness of the place haunted her.

Tears gathered in her eyes. "Let us go back, Papa. I don't want ChocoHearts."

She pulled his hand.

"Pest." His voice was harsh as he pushed her hands away from him. She stopped walking, and so did he. It was a small but deserted street. Mr Shikhar turned to the other end and waited for someone.

Walking towards them was a man who was much taller than Mr Shikhar. He had a thick moustache and broad shoulders, and his face was partly covered with a beard. His blue shirt was torn, and he was chewing betel leaves.

"Shanaya . . . come, be a dear. This uncle knows a better shop where ChocoHearts are available. Go with him," Mr Shikhar said.

She was frightened. "I don't want anything, and I don't want to go with him either."

"Don't be a fool, girl," Mr Shikhar warned her. But she stood stubbornly.

"Please take me back to my mother," she begged.

The other guy came forward. "I don't care about the emotional drama, mate. I don't have time for it."

Mr Shikhar nodded in exasperation. "I understand, but she does not."

He pushed Shanaya towards the other guy.

Holding the girl with one hand, the man informed Mr Shikhar dryly, "You know where to get your money. And forget about her. If you ever come back—"

"I will not." Mr Shikhar laughed.

"Good." The ruffian dragged the seven-year-old Shanaya away.

Mr Shikhar smiled. His job was done. He was going to get a hefty chunk of money. He just had to tackle a silly woman at home.

CHAPTER ELEVEN

A Miserable Childhood

When the odds are stacked against you, struggle but don't
run. Putting effort matters. Fight it out; whether you
hit or miss, you'll end up with the satisfaction that
you gave it your best shot.

***

"Papa!" Shanaya cried, but her plea went unanswered. Her stepfather did not even turn back to look at her.

"Mr Shikhar!"

The ruffian dragged the girl forcefully in the opposite direction. She tugged at the man's hands. "Uncle, where are you taking me?"

Giving her a weird look, the man ignored her question and briskly moved forward. There were no streetlights and it was dark. She was frightened. Not giving up, she made an effort to loosen his hold on her forcibly. That irritated the big man.

When she repeatedly tried to make him release his hold, he turned towards her and slapped her hard on the cheek.

"Ouch!" she cried, falling to the other end of the road. Mud splashed on her. As she staggered to get up, he dragged her by her plaited hair and pushed her ahead as Shanaya screamed in pain.

"Stop shouting, you brat!"

"Please let go of me, Uncle, or else!" she threatened.

"Or else what?" He laughed.

"I'll hit you!" Her soft voice was shrill.

"Hmm, please go ahead," he invited her, bending down to her height while still holding her plait.

Shanaya itched to hit him, but her hands shivered.

"Coward," he criticised her.

That forced her to slap his cheeks with the full vigour of a little girl.

"Stupid brat. What did you hope to achieve?" he sneered as he saw the fear in her eyes. "But it is payback time, kiddo. I am not about to lose to a little girl."

With those words, he began thrashing her. She wobbled in pain. Her cheeks throbbed where the rowdy man hit her mercilessly. His fat golden ring tore the edge of her lips. Blood oozed out.

"Shut your mouth. I don't have the patience to play with you," he warned.

A minivan was parked at the corner of the road. Opening the door at the back of the van, he pushed Shanaya inside. She stumbled forward as she heard the door shut with a bang before the van took off with them.

The driver's cabin was separated from the back of the

van by a barrier, and there was a small yellow light in one corner. There were two other kids, both of them almost her age, inside the van.

"Where are we going?" Shanaya asked the boy sitting opposite her. There was a girl at the other end of the minivan, but she was sleeping. Her eyes were partly closed.

The boy turned away, ignoring her question. He looked tired and his clothes were dirty and torn.

"Please," she requested.

He shrugged. "I don't know." He did not even look at her.

Shanaya whimpered, and that caught his attention.

He peered at her and noticed the red gash near her lips. "Did he hit you?"

Shanaya nodded.

"He is cruel," he remarked.

He touched her wound.

"Ouch!" she cried out.

"Does it hurt?"

"Yes." She shivered.

"Say yes to whatever he says. If you do that, he will not hit you," he advised her.

She agreed. "What is your name?"

"Mayank."

"I am Shanaya. How old are you, Mayank?"

"Eight."

"I am just seven," she muttered childishly, as if it was a sin to be so young.

"That is okay. I am older, and I can take care of you," he promised.

The friendship blossomed in the least expected of places.

"But where are they taking us?" she asked Mayank.

"Not sure." He strained to recollect what the big guys had spoken about earlier.

"I don't understand this," exclaimed Shanaya.

"Neither do I understand it completely . . . but I believe they will beat us again."

"Why?" She opened her eyes wide in anxiety.

"They will make us beg on the streets. If we don't obey them, they will hit us. . . if we still resist them, then they will puncture our eyes."

"We wouldn't be able to see then!" Shanaya shivered.

He nodded as they spoke like adults.

"But how do you know all this?"

"Before they put me in this van, I was kept in another room somewhere. There were other children there. One was blind. I asked him why he had been blinded, and he told me about what they did."

Shanaya trembled in fear. She felt cold and shouted, "Ma, save me from all this!"

"Don't shout, Shanaya. He might come back," Mayank warned her.

That stopped her.

"But how did you get into this?" he asked.

"My papa gave me to him."

"Your papa?" Mayank stammered.

"No . . . not my real one. He is Mr Shikhar . . . my real papa loved me."

The little boy nodded thoughtfully. The past week had exposed him to the cruelties on this earth.

"We have to get out of this," she spoke determinedly.

"What can we do? We need someone older to help us." He thought about it.

"Yes."

"But we can't trust anyone!" exclaimed Mayank.

"No, Mayank. Not everyone is bad," she said.

The van screeched to a halt. They had entered a dark warehouse. The driver and the ruffian dragged the three kids out of the van and thrust them into the building. Cobwebs fluttered everywhere. It was dark, and the lighting was minimal. They put them in a room full of kids.

"Earlier, I was in another room. That is where I met the blind boy. I don't know why they keep moving me to different places. I am scared," Mayank whispered to Shanaya.

The driver brought out a packet of bread. He threw the slices at the children as if they were dogs. There were just twelve pieces of bread, while there were at least twenty-five kids in the room. Shanaya did her math right.

"Mayank, no one will get more than half a slice of bread," she whispered.

"That is their plan," he murmured back.

But their conversation caught the attention of the ruffian.

"How dare you? Stay silent, you fool!" he shouted at Shanaya and pushed her towards one of the walls of the room. Not anticipating the push, she hit the wall.

Shanaya stood up moaning and had tears in her eyes. Her head had a painful reddish mark where it had hit the wall. The kids fought for the bread pieces.

"Should we get one more packet?" the driver asked the other guy.

The ruffian turned to him. "Are you mad? They have to look like starved kids for the people to show them pity and offer some money. We are just feeding them so that they don't die of hunger."

The kids shrank back at their tone and were ready to do anything at their command. The men strode out, closing the door with a bang.

Mayank ran to Shanaya. "Are you okay?"

She held her head tightly. "Yes, I am."

"Don't worry, Shanaya . . . let me see," volunteered Mayank, noticing her pain despite the assurance.

The corner of her head pounded in pain. Dizziness gripped her. "Relax, girl," the boy told her.

He ran to bring a tumbler of water from an old pot kept at the other end of the room. "Here, have this."

Shanaya looked at the dirty water.

"Please drink it. We have no other option," he cajoled as he saw that there was no other source of water in the room. Shanaya drank the water as the giddiness subsided gradually. He washed her wound with water.

A week passed by. The children suffered the same plight each day—half a slice of bread at times and a pot of dirty water. By now, they were all familiar with the other children there.

"They are preparing us," the bigger kids told the smaller ones.

"Are there only two people, Ritu?" Shanaya asked the girl who had been brought to the warehouse much earlier. Mayank was staring at a wall aimlessly.

"I have only seen these two. I don't know who else is with them. But I have heard them talking to many people over the phone through the window. When they found me watching them, they hit me. They have kept the window shut ever since then."

Shanaya nodded in sympathy.

"We don't have much time. They are planning to take us to the streets soon. We have to get out of here before that," she told them.

All the kids sat around her. Somehow, Shanaya had managed to emerge as the leader of the group. They trusted her implicitly. She made sure that the room was clean for them to sleep in. With the twigs and branches scattered around the place, she had made a small broom and would sweep the floor every day, piling up the dirt in a corner. She interacted with all the children and made them feel safe with her moral support.

They heard the scuffing sound of shoes. The kids scrambled away from each other. Someone unlocked the door. The ruffian was back with a pack of bread. The driver was not with him today. Shanaya's stomach rumbled in hunger. She had become thinner, and her eyes appeared big as her face had become considerably leaner.

Silence welcomed the ruffian, as a thread of fear ran through the children. The bread pieces flew here and there. Shanaya got half a piece of bread, which she finished within seconds. She was famished. Mayank looked at her with pity.

She did not fight for her food like the others. She ate only if she was able to catch a slice of bread in her hand.

"I think you are ready. All set to face the world and bring us money!" He laughed harshly. "And if you are not, then I will move you to another sector; organs are in demand now. It will pay us more, but it involves certain risks."

He sighed in exasperation. "So, brats, be prepared to beg." Observing everyone with satisfaction, he left the place.

Shanaya collapsed on the floor as the rowdy man closed the door.

Mayank ran to her. "Shanaya, wake up. I know you are hungry. Here, take my bread," he told her, shaking her. But she was cold and did not exhibit any reaction.

Her condition frightened the other kids.

"Wake up, Shanaya!" Mayank shouted.

Ritu did the same. The other kids gathered around them.

Mayank rushed to the door and hit it with full vigour. "Uncle, please come back! Shanaya is sick!"

He thumped the door again. The other kids joined him, understanding the urgency of the situation. The ruffian came back cursing.

"Brats! Why did you disturb me?"

"Uncle!" Mayank's voice faltered as he took note of his ferocious eyes.

"Be quick!" the man barked.

"Shanaya is not waking up. Is she dead?" Mayank asked him.

"What? We need all the brats . . . if not, we can't get our money as planned." He scowled as he pushed the kids out of his way.

Shanaya had crept closer to the door when no one was looking at her. As the man bent forward to check on her, she threw a handful of piled-up dust into his eyes and scrambled back, afraid that he might catch her. The man fell back with a thud, holding his eyes with both his hands.

He screamed as he lost his sense of direction and hit the wall of the room and fell down. Shanaya signalled to the other kids at that exact moment. Six kids encircled him and hit him hard as he struggled to get up.

"Run, everyone!" she shouted.

The ruffian growled as the kids scampered around him and he wriggled on the ground with his eyes partly closed.

"No time to waste," Shanaya instructed the children. As if on cue, they ran out of the room. Mayank held Shanaya's hands as they ran out last, ensuring that all the kids were out of the room.

The kids ran in different directions. It took the ruffian fifteen minutes to get back on his feet. Realising that he had lost all the kids, his anger turned venomous, and he marched straight to Shanaya's home to catch hold of Mr Shikhar.

"You will not get away with this, Shikhar!" he screamed in frustration.

Shanaya and Mayank ran until their legs ached.

"I can't run anymore, Mayank," she told him.

"Shanaya, please keep running; we don't know if that bad uncle is still chasing us," his childish voice warned her.

"But we are lost. Where are we? Where are the other kids? These roads are not familiar to me," she muttered in frustration.

"We are close to my home. I know this way."

"Mayank, let me come with you, please. I am scared of Mr Shikhar," she begged him.

"You can come with me. We will talk to my mother. She will be worried about me. But we can't keep waiting here," he answered her.

They walked on, panting and taking heavy breaths in between. Shanaya was about to give up, when Mayank shouted, "Hurray! We've done it, Shanaya! That is my home!"

That statement was enough to release adrenalin into their veins and they ran towards safety. A couple of policemen were standing outside, involved in a deep discussion. They were shocked to see the kids.

Mayank's mother was astonished to see her son after two long weeks. Dropping the container she had in her hands, she rushed to him. "Mayank! My dear boy! Where were you? Are you all right?" she cried.

Shanaya stepped back, longing to feel her mother's arms around herself. She missed her badly, but she was happy for her new friend.

Mayank's face became wet with happy tears.

"I thought I would never see you again, Ma," he cried.

She nodded in understanding. "I missed you too, baby. But what happened? Where did you go? Who took you?"

The policemen barged in, cutting their conversation short. They took Shanaya and Mayank, along with his parents, for a detailed enquiry about what had happened.

They told them whatever they knew. With the information from the kids, they had enough leads to progress with their investigation.

"Where are your parents? Where do you stay?" they asked Shanaya.

She told them about Mr Shikhar. "I don't want to go back to him, sir. But I want to meet my mother."

Understanding that Mr Shikhar could be a major witness in this case, they went to get her parents. The children waited for an hour and were given some milk and bread in the meantime.

"I am proud of you, little girl . . . you saved the lives of many kids," one of the policemen praised Shanaya.

"Thanks, Uncle," she muttered, dreading the thought of meeting Mr Shikhar again.

The policemen who had gone to bring back Shanaya's parents to the police station returned empty-handed. The inspector looked at them questioningly. They confirmed his suspicions wordlessly. Shanaya's parents had been found dead. The criminals had murdered Mr Shikhar and his wife to cover up their tracks. The inspector looked at the girl with sympathy.

"Shanaya . . . you need not meet Mr Shikhar again, ever," he told her on a positive note.

Her face brightened up instantly. "But my mother . . ." she asked.

"Be strong, Shanaya . . . your mother is safe with your papa."

"Does it mean . . . she is dead like my papa?" Her voice trembled.

He nodded in sympathy.

The inspector turned to Mayank and his parents, who were watching everything with compassion. "You can leave with your son. We have all the information now."

"But Shanaya?" Mayank's father questioned.

"Don't worry. We will take care of this little girl," the inspector promised. With that assurance, Mayank's family left the police station.

Later, after the legal formalities, the inspector handed Shanaya over to Mr and Mrs Dixit, who adopted her, admiring her bravery and beauty.

Most of all, she satisfied their craving for having a child that they had longed for all their lives.

CHAPTER TWELVE

The College Drama

The best combo in this world is a cup of coffee with your best friend. The caffeine, blended with friendship, is powerful enough to dissolve your troubles and kick-start you in a matter of seconds.

***

Days passed by. Shanaya came to understand that she was extremely lucky to have broken out of the circle of human trafficking, where the kids were sold as slaves for begging or sexual exploitation or even for organ harvesting. The police had broken the small racket, all thanks to the information provided by them. She shuddered as she recollected what a close call it had been.

She was eternally grateful to the Dixit family. Given a chance to return their care, she would do anything for them. She was provided with all the worldly goodies, right from pretty gowns to the best education in Delhi.

At times, her memories about her papa and the ChocoHearts he was supposed to get for her taunted her. She tried her best to bury those memories inside her soul. She was never meant for ChocoHearts. Mr Dixit took her to multiple counselling sessions to overcome her childhood trauma. The longing for her old family caused an invisible barrier between her and the Dixits. But they understood her feelings and did not push her for more than what she could give.

Years went by. Shanaya was now a college student.

She completed her engineering without any hiccups. She had friends of her own and her world became colourful. She believed that she had found her soulmate in her best friend, Sakshi. It was only when they both opted for a post-graduation degree in Business Administration that life became problematic once again.

The day began as an ordinary one. Shanaya dressed in a knee-length pencil skirt with a white tank top for the day. She bound her hair into a high ponytail and wore shoes made of a soft velvet. With a tint of red gloss on her lips and a pair of rhinestone earrings, she looked stunning.

"Wow, Shanaya, you look gorgeous!" Sakshi complimented her as she stepped into the class.

"You too, Sakshi," she returned the compliment. Shanaya noted that Sakshi looked very feminine in her knee-length blue dress, embroidered at the top.

Sakshi smiled. Initially, the seed of a friendship had been planted between them when they were introduced in the first year of their engineering course, but now it had sprouted and grown into a big tree.

The roots had grown deeper over the years, strengthening their bond. They were the best of buddies and shared almost everything under the sun.

"Sakshi, I don't see you nowadays," Shanaya complained.

Her friend coloured.

"Hmm, interesting . . . why does my dear friend blush? Has she got something to hide?" Shanaya taunted.

"As if I can hide things from you! You are Sherlock Holmes," she retorted, but her eyes failed to meet Shanaya's.

"Yes, you can." Shanaya laughed at Sakshi.

The other girl pouted, ignoring her.

"Come on; don't be a dark horse, Sakshi. I rang you up multiple times yesterday, but your phone was always engaged. Whom were you talking to?"

"If someone else had asked me this, I would say, 'Mind your own business'."

"You can't say that to me. So, cut out your evasive replies and let me in on the secret," teased Shanaya.

"Okay, I confess. I met someone." She raised her hands.

"Met?"

"I met him during our last year of engineering."

"Oh. You did not tell me, Sakshi . . . and here I was thinking we don't have any secrets between us," complained Shanaya.

"I wanted to tell you, Shan, but I waited to confirm whether or not he was the one for me."

"What is the conclusion then?"

"Yes, he is the man for me."

"Wow, you made such a strong statement, Sakshi. I want to meet the person who has made such an impact on my beautiful friend."

"He is our senior," added Sakshi.

"Oh . . . do I know him?" asked Shanaya.

"I am not sure you would have seen him. You never look at the boys even though the entire college drools over your beauty." She laughed.

Shanaya stared at her in mock anger. "You are exaggerating!"

"No, Shan. It is true. But you have never even given them a single glance. They have nicknamed you the Ice Queen, you are so haughty and all."

"Oh my!" she laughed. The nickname did not bother her.

"I would have wept buckets over the name. But you have faced scenarios worse than this," concluded Sakshi.

Shanaya agreed. "You changed the track of our conversation. I want to meet your hero."

"Okay. I will take you along today. Let us catch up with him at Spring Garden after class."

"Deal." Shanaya shook hands happily with her friend.

***

Shanaya looked at her watch for the fifth time. Sakshi had told her that she would join her after a little makeover. She wanted to look fresh and vibrant when her guy saw her. Though they had not declared their love for each other, Sakshi was expecting a proposal from him any time, and she wanted to be prepared for it and look her best.

She joined Shanaya with an apologetic smile. It was a small park and they soon heard the sound of a bike stopping outside.

"Oh God, it is him!" Sakshi exclaimed. "Do I look okay?"

"Sakshi, you are pretty," Shanaya told her in exasperation. But she was curious to see the person who had made Sakshi go nuts about him. A familiar face walked towards them.

Shanaya frowned. "Hello, Sakshi," the guy wished.

He wrinkled his eyebrows when he saw Shanaya. The same wave of familiarity hit him as well.

Not noticing their reactions, Sakshi went ahead to introduce them. But they completed the introductions themselves.

"Shanaya," stammered Mayank.

"Mayank," she muttered.

Sakshi looked at them in confusion. Then realisation dawned upon her as she recollected Shanaya's past. "Oh Shan, don't tell me that Mayank is the same little boy who helped you years ago!"

Silence claimed them for a few seconds.

Shanaya did not contradict Sakshi's words.

"Oh God, it really is you, Shanaya . . . I can't believe my eyes," whispered Mayank.

Shanaya looked at the physically well-built Mayank, who stood six feet tall with a well-sculpted body. She could understand why Sakshi had fallen for him. In his red striped T-shirt and blue jeans, he looked like a hero who had stepped right out of a Bollywood movie.

"The same here," confessed Shanaya, glad that she was able to connect with Mayank after a long time. Their last meeting had been at the police station when she was seven years old.

"You have grown into a beautiful girl," he complimented her.

Noting the way his compliment disturbed Sakshi, Shanaya added, "Not as pretty as Sakshi though."

"How did I miss seeing you?" he asked Shanaya.

"Mayank, you joined this college last year for your MBA, and Shanaya never looks at any boy in college," said Sakshi.

"Are you the *Ice Queen Shanaya* then? Oh my God! I never connected the dots!"

"What is there to connect?" Sakshi frowned at their shared thread of familiarity.

But Shanaya's attitude comforted Sakshi, and soon they became the best of friends. The trio became inseparable the entire year. Together, they went to the movies and had fun. They roamed around every nook and corner of Delhi. They did their shopping together and ate at all the street shops. Not a day went by without them having *pani puris*[7] at some roadside food stall or the other. A few of the students believed that the Ice Queen had melted for Mayank.

The year was about to end, and the girls understood that Mayank would be leaving soon as he was in his final year.

---

7   One of the most popular Indian street foods, *pani puri* is a fried crisp *puri* (a type of unleavened bread from India and Pakistan, usually deep-fried) filled with a lip-smacking potato preparation and loaded with flavourful water!

The day of his farewell dawned. Both of Sakshi and Shanaya were dressed in beautiful sarees to celebrate—Shanaya in red and Sakshi in blue. They had the usual festivities in the college with the entire class. In the evening, the three of them walked towards their favourite pani puri shop to have their private celebrations.

Mayank smiled at them. Sakshi's heart fluttered, fervently hoping that her relationship with Mayank would be taken to the next level that day.

"Sakshi, be a dear and get us a bottle of mineral water from the corner shop," requested Mayank.

"How can I say no to my hero?" She was open with her compliment. The moment she was out of earshot, Mayank turned to Shanaya.

"Shanaya," he called.

She turned towards him, observing Sakshi hopping happily.

"I have feelings for you . . ."

She froze at his words. "What are you talking about, Mayank?"

"I will miss you when I leave this college."

"Yeah. You will miss Sakshi more." Her voice forced him to confirm.

"Yes, I will miss Sakshi, but only as a friend . . . but with you, it is different," he replied.

"Sakshi loves you, Mayank," she told him fiercely.

"But I love you, Shanaya. I love your courage . . . the way you fought against those rowdy men even at such a young age . . . your beauty, your intelligence . . . your everything."

"I am not going to encourage this, Mayank." Shanaya was firm.

"You can't force me to live with Sakshi," he retorted.

She shook her head. "I never expected this from you . . . I won't poach on my best friend's boyfriend," she whispered.

"It is not like that. I have never proposed to her," he denied.

"But you encouraged her . . . you made her believe that you like her."

"So did you," he criticised.

Their angry conversation was interrupted by Sakshi, who had returned with a bottle of water, unaware of the undercurrents that passed between them.

The day ended quickly after that fiery conversation, as they did not want to prolong the uneasiness that had settled between them. Mayank left soon. Sakshi complained to Shanaya, "I thought he would propose to me, Shanaya . . . but he did not."

She cried after Mayank left.

"Don't worry, Sakshi. He will understand your love soon," Shanaya consoled her. It took Shanaya almost half an hour to calm her and send her back home.

The academic year ended, and Mayank left to join the corporate world in Noida. He accepted the job offer from an MNC, which he had received during the campus placement. Shanaya cut off contact with him completely. She thought it was best for all three of them. She responded to neither his calls nor his messages. She even ignored him on the road when he came to meet her.

Sakshi met Mayank frequently at his new company. Shanaya never joined her. She did not want to stand in her friend's way. Also, she did not want to give Mayank an opportunity to criticise her by saying that she had encouraged him. She did not want him to misconstrue her friendship. The second year passed off without any mishaps for the girls. They passed with flying colours, and both of them had offer letters from multinational companies.

Sakshi was ecstatic as she managed to get a job in the same company as Mayank. She joined there as a trainee initially. Shanaya got a call from Sakshi after a month.

"Hi Shanaya, how are you?"

"Good . . . how are you, Sakshi?"

"I am enjoying things as usual . . . have you taken up the offer from ANZ?" she asked Shanaya.

"Yes, and it is going great . . ."

Before Shanaya could complete her answer, Sakshi continued excitedly. "It is Mayank's birthday tomorrow. I am planning a small birthday celebration tonight . . . just the three of us at my place, like we used to."

Shanaya was about to decline the invitation when Sakshi interrupted her, "Please don't say no. I want to take a trip down our beautiful memory lane, Shanaya . . . you have become so busy these days." Not wanting to hurt her feelings, Shanaya reluctantly accepted her invitation.

***

Taking a deep breath, Shanaya walked into Sakshi's home. Her parents welcomed her with a warm smile and sent her up to the terrace, where Sakshi had arranged everything to perfection. Setting up the cake at the centre of the table, Sakshi turned to Shanaya, "Hey girl, I am happy to see you after such a long time." She hugged her exuberantly.

"Happy to see you too, dear. The arrangement is perfect, Sakshi. Mayank is lucky," she commented.

"I am setting up the environment for his proposal, Shanaya. I will be the luckiest person in this world if he proposes to me. I have waited for him for more than two years, Shan. I can't wait anymore," she confessed.

Mayank joined the celebration soon, but his eyes were only on Shanaya.

"Hello, Shanaya . . . how are you?" His voice was husky.

"Good," she murmured, turning away.

Sakshi complained, "Mayank, you did not comment on the decoration."

"It is beautiful, Sakshi. Thanks for arranging all this," he told her dutifully.

"We shall cut the cake then," she told him.

"Shouldn't we call Uncle and Aunty?" Shanaya suggested.

"I have already told them about what I have planned. They said they will not gatecrash our private party," replied Sakshi, winking.

She dragged Mayank towards the cake. Mayank sliced the cake as they sang the birthday song for him. Taking a piece of the cake, he went ahead to feed Shanaya.

Sakshi was stunned.

Shanaya muttered, "Don't do this, Mayank! Sakshi deserves better." She declined the cake, stepping back.

"Okay, you don't want the cake. That is fine with me. Could you please accept this at least?"

With those words, Mayank took a box out of his pocket and opened it to reveal a beautiful ring inside. "I love you, Shanaya."

Sakshi cried out sharply. Shanaya closed her eyes in frustration. She had not wanted this to happen.

"No, Mayank!"

He held her shoulders to stop her from going back. Slow in grasping things around her, Sakshi finally understood what Mayank was doing. Her heart shattered and her emotions went haywire.

Shanaya stood silent as Sakshi came towards them. Her anger turned towards her. "Trust . . . don't you know the meaning of the word, Shanaya?"

"I did not—"

"You destroyed my trust, Shanaya. You backstabbed me!"

"No, Sakshi . . . I did not. Please, you've got to believe me."

Mayank stepped in between the two of them. "It is not the way you think, Sakshi."

Her fury multiplied at the way Mayank defended Shanaya. She continued venomously, "Did you not have any inkling that Mayank was about to propose to you?"

She observed Shanaya as a wave of guilt passed her face.

"I have my answer. You are disgusting, Shanaya. You behaved so cheaply," Sakshi condemned her.

"Enough, Sakshi," Mayank stopped her.

"Don't you dare support her!" she shouted at him.

"Hit me, Sakshi, if that will make you feel better," invited Shanaya in a dull tone.

"Hit you? I will not even touch a scumbag like you!" She laughed harshly to cover the sadness that threatened to overwhelm her.

"You don't understand, Sakshi," Mayank tried to elaborate as he held Shanaya with one hand.

"No, stop it!" Shanaya shouted. Tugging her hands forcefully from Mayank's, she felt awful for hurting their feelings.

She took the wedding invitation out of her handbag. "I am sorry, Mayank. This is the answer to your proposal. I am engaged to be married. I thought of inviting you both to my wedding. But the situation here went out of control."

Mayank stopped her. "Don't do this, Shanaya."

She turned to him with angry tears in her eyes. "I will if it pleases my family. And you have to apologise to Sakshi. You have treated her badly. You don't deserve her love, Mayank. You don't deserve her."

Shanaya stormed out, taking her bag with her and stuffing the invitation inside. The situation did not appear conducive enough anymore for her to share her wedding invitation with her friends. She ran away from Sakshi's house before they could stop her. Love was blind. Shanaya understood that she had to pay for Mayank's mistakes. She had become the culprit in her friend's opinion. Sakshi would blame only her. Shanaya knew her very well. With her love-struck eyes, she would neither criticise Mayank nor find fault with him. Shanaya prayed fervently that Mayank realised the love that Sakshi had for him and came to his senses. But her friendship with Sakshi was destroyed irrevocably. It was dead.

***

Sakshi paused for a moment before completing her story.

"That was the last time I saw her," she narrated.

Siddharth had tears in his eyes when he came back to the present. His heart hurt at the thought of Shanaya suffering. His cheeks were wet, and Sakshi suspected that he had cried throughout.

"You can't blame Shanaya for your break-up, Sakshi. It was Mayank's mistake."

"You might be right," she told him in regret.

"Is he married?"

"No, not yet. I have a feeling that he is still waiting for Shanaya."

"But she is already married. She will not go back to him," he denied harshly.

"How do you know that?"

"I am her husband, Sakshi."

She was stunned. There was a knock on the door just then.

"Come in," invited Siddharth.

Shanaya walked in. She was surprised to see Sakshi in Sid's cabin. Feeling guilty over the way she had treated Shanaya, Sakshi left the cabin without a word, leaving a bewildered Shanaya with Siddharth.

CHAPTER THIRTEEN

The Chase

*Marriage is not just about the grandeur of the day
with the gorgeous lehengas, scrumptious food, and fresh
mehendi. It is about how the couple fight for their
relationship to hold the fort of love.*

***

"What was she doing here?"

Siddharth turned to Shanaya, acting all innocent. "Are you referring to Sakshi?"

"Who else?" Shanaya nodded.

"She is a new employee at *India-Bliss*. She is in marketing and sales."

"Same region as mine?" she queried, hoping that Siddharth would reply in the negative.

"No. For the northern region."

"Okay then," she said.

"Do you know her, Shanaya?"

Her eyes darkened with the bad memories, but she shook her head. "Not really."

"But she knows you well," Sid added as he watched her reaction. She froze for a couple of seconds. Wiping away all the emotions from her face, she placed a few files on his desk.

"Sign them, please."

He gazed at Shanaya with sympathy as he thought of her horrible childhood. How frightened she must have been when her stepfather had cheated her. If he was murdered, then the fellow deserved it. To Sid, he was a traitor who had played on the feelings of a seven-year-old girl. On top of it, Shanaya had lost her mother in that whole fiasco. Despite those mishaps, she had faced life confidently. Never once in her life had she cowered before her problems. She deserved nothing but unconditional love. All his issues appeared insignificant when he compared them with what she had gone through.

His eyes were wet.

"Are you crying, Sid?"

Wordlessly, he dropped the pen in his hand back into the file and came forward to hug her tight. She was astonished. The cabin door was closed, but still, anyone could walk in at any moment.

"Sid . . ."

She tried to step back.

"No . . . please stay," he told her without loosening his hold. The warmth of his voice calmed her. His fingers gently ruffled her hair.

"You deserve happiness, Shanaya."

"I don't deny that, but if this has anything to do with what I assume Sakshi must have told you, then I don't need your pity." She tried to brush his words off with a grin.

"Shh!" He put his fingers over her lips and held her tightly against him, trying to take away her sorrows with his support. "I mean it. No one in this world deserves it more than you."

She frowned. She did not need Sid's sympathy if he felt badly about her past.

"I deserve happiness, boss . . . but also the signatures," she insisted, coming out of his hug.

He laughed, breaking the moment to sign the rest of the files. She was captivated by his smile.

"Please smile more often," she murmured.

"I will," he promised, envisaging a happy future after a long time.

He watched her as she left his cabin, taking the signed files with her. Wearing a blue and pink salwar, he knew that she was the prettiest woman in the office. She was bold, beautiful, intelligent, and, most of all, she was his. She was his wife! She was Mrs Shanaya Saxena. The possessive feeling that brimmed inside him when he thought about Shanaya tugged at his heart. It was overpowering enough to consume him, but the good thing was that it did not pull him down; instead, it lifted his spirits and brightened his mood.

Realisation dawned upon Sid. His feelings for Mishti paled into insignificance. Shock rocked him. What he had thought was love for Mishti had never been love. The fact had stared at him all along, but he had been blind to it. It had been mere attraction from both sides. If it had been true love, they would have fought for their relationship and not given up in the name of fate. But they had done just that. However, Shanaya never gave up. She had put in more than one hundred per cent into their relationship, even though she had never had any proper response from his end. He did not know when it had happened, but he had feelings for his wife.

Would Shanaya reciprocate? Or did she still have feelings for that stupid Mayank? Rationally, he realised that the childhood tragedy Shanaya and Mayank had shared together had created a special bond between them. But would she break their marital relationship over that? A feeling of jealousy ripped through him.

He wanted to call her back and hug her again. Smiling at the thought, he murmured, "Beware, Shan . . . the chase has begun. You are mine, and I will show you what love is as you showed me."

***

Sid entered his home. It was five in the evening. Having reached earlier, Shanaya beamed warmly as she went to him. He was proud that he was the recipient of such a beautiful smile.

Acknowledging her with a salute, he went to freshen up and came to the dining hall in his casual wear. It was snack time.

A glass container caught his attention. "Wow, paneer rolls! What is the occasion?"

"Nothing. I thought you needed some cheering up. You appeared dull at the office, so I made them for you," she answered.

"Why do you care for me so much?" His question was direct as he gazed into her eyes, taking a bite of the delicacy.

She flushed. "Why do you make a big deal out of a simple snack?"

"Tsk!" He pursed his lips. "The snack doesn't matter, my dear wife. The intention matters, and the fact that you made it matters more to me."

"Wah! You are boring me, boss. Finish it," she said as her heart fluttered at his acknowledgement.

"I am not your boss at home, Shanaya." His voice was stern. She did not know what to make of his behaviour. "I promise to finish it. But tell me . . . why did you not share your childhood story with me?"

Unable to hold his gaze, she lowered her head and muttered, "What is there to share? Nothing enchanting . . ."

He kept looking into her eyes, willing her to tell the truth.

"I know . . . Sakshi must have told you everything."

"Yes."

What else had Sakshi told him? She was unsure as they had not parted on the best of terms.

"There was nothing much to say, Sid . . . I had a tough phase in my life, but it passed and I moved on. And life has been beautiful after I moved in with the Dixit family."

"Now you are a Saxena." He was quick to point out.

"Yes, and I am all the more happy!" she exclaimed.

"Really?"

"Yes, and cut that protective look. I am made of sterner stuff than you think."

"I know that," agreed Sid.

Shanaya doubted that, and it showed on her face. Sid never could control his urge to protect her. She was about to retaliate, when he informed her, "Shan, I almost forgot. My mother has sent something for you. Here you go."

Taking a gift-wrapped package out of his office bag, which was lying on the table, he passed it to her. She was surprised. What had Sita Aunty sent?

Unwrapping the parcel, she found herself staring at a gorgeous satin saree with a custom-made blouse. It was well designed with an embroidered black border against the softness of the blue material. Pearls shaped as flowers were stitched into the corners.

She gasped at its beauty. "It is stunning! It looks as if she made this specially for me. I have to call her."

"No, that is okay. I will tell her. Why don't you wear it? Let us go out for dinner."

"But I was planning to make you rotis. I gave Varuna the day off. She appeared sick," she said.

"You did a good thing. But don't stress about cooking. Let us relax. By the way, the paneer rolls were delicious. Save the rest for tomorrow. Now go and get ready," he instructed her.

"Aye aye, captain!" She giggled and rushed off to try her new saree. His happy mood caught up with her. Half an hour passed by.

The moment she stepped into the living room again, all dressed up, Siddharth whistled involuntarily.

"You are stunning, Shan."

She blushed at his compliment.

Sid did not exaggerate. The saree fit her like second skin, enhancing her curves, and hinted at what he was missing out on. His eyes did not miss out on any small detail—her tiny gold earrings, the broad butterfly-shaped bracelet around her wrist, and the little bindi[8] on her forehead.

He moved close to her. "Just one more thing . . ."

He released the tortoiseshell clasp that held her hair in a tight ponytail.

"What are you doing?" she gasped, trying to tame her chaotic hair.

"Let your hair free, Shanaya. It suits you."

Rebelling a little, she tried to tie her hair back. Moving closer still, he held her hands tightly with one of his. "No, don't. Let it be this way."

Shanaya blinked at his words.

"Don't be so uptight, Shan . . . there are times when you have to let go. It is not necessary to always do the right thing."

His mesmerising words teased her. Siddharth was driving her insane. Her eyes widened as she noted how close they stood against each other. Their bodies brushed and waves of heat engulfed her, tingling her feet. A sweet sensation filled her. Their eyes attracted each other like magnets, and desire blazed like a piece of red-hot coal.

---

8   A small coloured mark or jewel that is worn on the forehead, between the eyebrows, especially by Hindu women to show that they are married.

"Please don't," she whispered, begging him to stop before they had even started.

"Don't what, my dear wife?"

"Touch me . . ." Her voice was husky.

"I will not promise . . . but I'll try."

Lifting her hands, Siddharth pushed her gently against the pale-yellow wall behind her and she felt its hardness against her back. Inches away, he bent a little and inhaled the fragrance of her hair.

"A divine aroma . . ." His voice was thick as he ran his fingers through her silky hair. She quivered as he played gently with her black strands.

"Sid . . ." she whispered.

Tenderly, he blew a lock of hair away from her forehead. His lips almost touched hers, and she shuddered.

"This is better," he told her calmly, leaving her burning inside.

A mischievous mood took over her, and she looked at him with seductive eyes. With her black winged brows and pink lips, she was all game, dressed in her killer saree. The mood was set.

"Let go," he had taunted her earlier.

Do I appear stuffy like a schoolmarm to him? I will make him take back his words . . .

Shanaya put her hand on Sid's shoulder and tilted his head a little as her fingers gripped his hair lightly. Tiptoeing up, she possessed his lips. An electric spark connected them, and his poised expression exploded. He held back with an incredulous query. "Shanaya?"

She nodded. He knew . . . and she knew that as well. Wordlessly, she claimed his surprised lips again. His mouth parted slightly and blood thundered through his veins. She curled into him as if it was the most natural thing in the world to do. They fit into each other like two halves melded into one. Her eyes were shut, but her soft lips explored his, knowing that they were surrounded by the insanity of ecstasy.

He was sure that she could hear his rapid heartbeat thumping in his chest. "Oh my God, Shan," he groaned as her kisses invaded his senses.

Losing his control, he held her hips with his left hand and dragged her forward to take control and taste the sweetest form of nectar, which seemed to fill her. His fingers caressed the softness of her arms, and his lips traced the contours of her face to reach the side of her neck. She came to her senses with a jolt as fire ripped through her senses.

"Siddharth . . . we have to leave." She pushed him away firmly, hoping that he would stop as things were beginning to get out of control. If he did not, she had to blame herself. She had started this.

"Oh my God . . . I am—"

She put a hand over his mouth. "Please don't apologise . . . let us go out for dinner. I am starving."

They were almost breathless and tried to contain their raging feelings. She did not want to dissect what had happened between them. She found it beautiful and wanted it to stay that way.

"I am not sorry that it happened, Shanaya . . . but you deserve better," Siddharth told her honestly. He had to woo her, court her, love her madly before getting into this. If Shanaya did not deserve these romantic trimmings, no one in this world did.

Acting as adults, they brushed these undercurrents under the carpet temporarily and proceeded to have a peaceful dinner, talking about all the silly things in the world.

***

Never in his life had Sid enjoyed such a wonderful dinner. Shanaya was a visual treat and a stimulating conversant on a wide variety of topics. It was a pleasure to spend time with her, and by the time they drove back home, she was exhausted. Leaning against him in the back seat, she had fallen asleep in a matter of seconds. He did not want to disturb her. Not really bothered about what their neighbours or his driver would think, he carried her from the car to their apartment. He unlocked the door and carried her safely to his room, where he gently put her on his bed. She stretched and made herself comfortable as her head sank into the softness of the pillow. He smiled as he stopped at the door. A sense of elation filled him to see her in his bed.

She woke up in an hour, when he cocooned her with the warmth of his quilt. Understanding that she was in his room, she sat up with a start.

"Why did you bring me here?" Shanaya demanded.

He frowned. "Why? Should you be asking your husband this?"

"Siddharth . . . please don't play games," she pleaded, her eyes open wide.

"Why would I play with you, Shanaya? I am serious," he told her solemnly.

Frightened, her eyes filled with tears, and she looked like she was about to explode any moment.

"Shan, relax . . . I was kidding! You are safe with me." He laughed. "Did you not see?" He pointed to a row of pillows that divided the spacious bed into two.

"So, you were playing with me all the time?"

"Who else can I play with?" Sid demanded.

"You deserve to be hit, Siddharth!" she yelled at him.

"There is no need to sleep in separate rooms, Shan . . . you can take the other end of the bed. Trust me. I will not cross this boundary. I just want you to be with me."

At her doubtful expression, he added, "If you still don't believe me, let me take the couch as I did in the earlier days of our marriage when Ma was here."

"No, it is okay. I trust you," she agreed. And even as the words popped out of her mouth, she realised that she truly trusted him and felt safe with him.

"But can I trust you? Or will you take advantage of a poor sleeping man?" he goaded her purposely.

Falling for the bait, she grabbed a flower vase nearby and threatened to hit him. Sid rushed out of the room laughing.

***

It was midnight. Sid's even breathing indicated that he was asleep. Shanaya had changed into white cotton pyjamas when she had woken up. She sat on the bed. Sleep eluded her. She watched Sid sleep peacefully as the moonlight filtered into the room through the curtains. Frustrated, she went to the kitchen to have a cup of milk. Taking her mobile out, she decided to leave a message for her mother-in-law so that she could see it first thing in the morning.

```
Thanks for the saree, Aunty. I loved
it.
```

She included a picture of her in the saree.

She knew that she would never forget the saree and the memories that they had created today. Even if she had to leave their home and Siddharth at some point, these moments would always stay in her heart.

The mobile vibrated. She was surprised that Sita Aunty was awake at this hour.

```
How are you, beti? I am confused. I
never sent you any saree. I have bought
a couple of kurtas for you. I will bring
them the next time I visit Bangalore.
You look awesome in the saree, but it
is not from me.
```

She scrolled through the messages. Did it mean that Siddharth had picked up the saree himself?

```
Oh, sorry, Aunty. I misunderstood.
Apologies for disturbing your sleep.
Good night.
```

She put the mobile back on the table next to the bed. She remembered the way Siddharth had stopped her from thanking his mom. It was a gift from him!

She was surprised, but happiness coursed through her. Was he really changing? Was he ready to be her husband at last, cutting off his emotional attachment with Mishti?

His tenderness was undoing her. She was falling for him deeply every day. It was becoming difficult to stay away from him. The worst part of it was that he was not letting her move away.

She tiptoed towards him. Bending over, she put her lips on his forehead. "Thanks for the gift, Sid. I loved it. It meant a lot to me," she whispered.

Siddharth shifted in his sleep. Quickly, she went back to her side of the bed as a wave of embarrassment swept over her. Closing her eyes, she waited for sleep to claim her.

CHAPTER FOURTEEN

The Push

Sometimes we just let life override us, traveling wherever it takes us; but don't always be a rider. Take the driver's seat and decide which way to go.

***

The following day, it was a disaster in the office. After the previous day's debacle, Shanaya felt that it was going to be tough to go back to the professional setup she had earlier with her husband. He had left early for office. There had been an urgent call from his father and he had to attend to it.

As she walked past the cubicles, she sensed that something was wrong. Hearing hushed whispers all around, she concluded that the matter was serious. One of the conversations she overheard between some women in the restroom bothered her. They were scared that the magazine would not survive and that they would lose their jobs soon. Sighing, she knocked on the door of Siddharth's cabin.

He frowned at the bunch of papers he was staring at. "Yes, come in," he called.

The familiar smell of Shanaya's vanilla perfume taunted him. "Good morning, Shanaya," he wished her without taking his eyes off the papers in his hand.

She sensed that he was disturbed with the situation.

"What is it, boss?" she asked him with concern. All she could see was the worried face of a CEO. There were no traces of the lover boy from the yesterday.

"The papers, Shan . . . take a look." He pointed to an article. She moved next to him and peered at the news item to understand the reason for all the commotion.

DailyNewsForAll, a popular newspaper, had predicted that *India-Bliss* would not survive beyond six months. With dropping sales, the magazine was forecasted to flop unless a miracle happened. There was also some criticism about how they had been unable to make it in the digital market.

"Damn!" Sid hit his fists against the table. "This will traumatise the employees and the shareholders too. The price of our stocks has dropped steeply today. That is why Dad called this morning."

"How dare they? We are doing our best, right Sid?" She was worried about their employees and their families.

"Yes. We have digitalised our magazines and newsletters. The sales, however, have dropped despite our digitisation. These papers are preying on that. But the decline in our sales has slowed down considerably."

Shanaya nodded, taking it all in.

"The worrying factor here is that there is no significant jump in the subscriptions, Shan," he stated in a worried tone.

"Did Raghu give you his analysis?"

"I am going through those reports. He is my only hope." Sid pulled the papers from underneath the news article.

"And what has he suggested?"

"He has built upon your suggestion, Shanaya . . . targeting people with simple one-liner news. We will try to understand their interests and target the right audience with the right news. He has sent tips on how to go about it."

"That sounds good," encouraged Shanaya.

"Good, but not great." He wrinkled his eyebrows.

"Why is that?"

"It is already being done in the market, Shan. We are not doing anything different," he pointed out.

"Don't worry, Sid. I know that you will figure out something else." She tapped him from the side, glancing at the reports herself.

"I must. No other option. If not, I'll end up putting the jobs of my employees at stake." He shook the feeling of negativity that threatened to overtake him. He had to stay strong.

Finally, he turned his attention completely to her. His eyes spotted a wrapped package in her hands. He grimaced.

"What is that?"

She smiled without a reply. That triggered his suspicion.

"Who is it for?" he asked dryly.

"My best friend."

"Rohit?"

"Rohit is my friend, yes, but this is for my best friend and my partner. Someone special. The one who gifted me with beautiful memories yesterday," she replied, swallowing her nervousness.

"Me?" He blinked. He had not expected that.

"Who else, sir? I am glad I brought this today," she said.

On that note, she gave him the gift.

"I am not in the mood for celebrations, Shanaya. Don't get me wrong if I don't appreciate what you have gotten for me."

"I understand, boss. But that will not happen."

He opened the gift and was astonished to see a plain gold bracelet engraved with a quote in cursive letters: *Your time will come!*

He stared at it for a long time. It was as if someone had foreseen his future. He could sense the positivity it emanated. He badly needed that to pull his people out of this rut. He smiled. Shanaya's gift touched his soul. He had needed that assurance from someone. She had read his mind to perfection, weaving magic around him, and it tied him in knots.

"It will. When did you get this?"

"I got this for you a long time back, when you began painting again. But I completely forgot about it. When I saw you leaving hurriedly after Dad's call, with a worried face, I thought you might require this assurance today."

He hugged her. "Thanks! It means a lot to me. But do you believe it?"

Shanaya nodded with absolute certainty. "How can I not? I know that you will not give up without a fight!"

She removed the clasp and took the bracelet out of the velvet bed on which it resided. Bending a little, she put it around his hand. "Your time will come," she repeated the words in a whisper. Both of them believed in it from their hearts. She pressed her lips on his hands and gave him the kiss of confidence and strength to go ahead.

The meaning of love hit him forcibly. He wanted to fight against all odds. Not crumble and wither into darkness. If life threw lemons at him, he knew that she would be there for him. And most of all, Shanaya believed and trusted that he could do it. He would do it for sure! He would prove it to her that her trust in him was not misplaced.

With renewed strength and determination, he said, "I do have an idea, but I need your help, Shanaya, for its execution."

"Ask me," she invited.

"I know you are good at writing. I am planning to use your skills here."

She looked confused, not getting his point.

"Can the novelist write micro-stories for us?"

"I don't get it."

"Look, Raghu has split our reader base into different segments. We know their exact interests, where they are from, what they like, what they read. We have our recent user-submitted survey results as well. That is golden information for us. Raghu's plan is to target our readers with one-liner news. But I suggest we splash not only the facts, but also fiction. One-line love stories for the teenagers, philosophical thoughts for people in their forties, baby tips for the moms in their early thirties, one-line investment strategies for the stock investors, and so on. But each piece of information that we publish should not cross ten words."

When Shanaya looked at him in awe, he continued, "People don't have the time and patience to read through a complete article like you said. Neither do we have enough time to captivate their minds with articles spanning two to three pages. The key strategy here is to capture their attention within a second so that they go ahead and subscribe with us."

She nodded, wholeheartedly convinced with the idea. "This is awesome, Sid. How did you get this idea?"

"I got it when I read a one-line story written by my favourite author, Ernest Hemingway—*For sale: Baby shoes. Never worn.* With six words, he had triggered a thread of sadness in my heart. That single line lingered on in my mind for more than a week. Such was the impact. I understood the power of words."

His plan made a lot of sense. "I will do my best, boss. You have to pay me extra."

"Deal." He shook hands with her.

"This is my forte, boss. You can rely on me," she said.

He smiled. "Please arrange an all-employee meeting in half an hour. Let the Bangalore employees attend in person. The rest can connect online. I have to reassure them so that they come out of the panic mode and give their best shot."

"Aye aye, boss. I took down notes about your plan. I will document it, prepare the reports, and organise meetings with the respective heads."

Sid shook his head. "Not required, Shanaya. I am removing you from your present role. You will be the editor of this new campaign for a month. Your entire focus will be on that. My assistant Prashit is back."

"Is his daughter all right?"

"She is doing absolutely fine. I am happy for her. For a moment, she had me scared when she was fighting that dreadful disease," he confessed.

She nodded sympathetically.

"Let us visit her sometime, Shanaya. I want you to meet her. She is a fighter like you."

His compliment made her proud. As if on cue, Prashit walked in. Shanaya passed on the information to him.

"Whom do I report to from now?" she asked.

Sid frowned. "Who else? ME. I'll be driving this campaign." He sounded possessive. Prashit glanced at them curiously.

***

After a busy day at work, Siddharth was late in returning home. Shanaya was watching television in the living room, keeping an eye on the door, expecting him any moment. It was almost eleven. He walked in, tired.

"Sid, your dinner has become cold. Let me warm it for you. You missed lunch as well," she complained, looking at his untouched lunchbox.

"You have become a nagging wife," he grumbled.

"I don't care what you call me. Take care of your health first," she ordered.

"Okay, ma'am." He saluted her even as his stomach rumbled with hunger. She laughed. He went to change into his nightclothes and was back in a flash after a quick wash.

Silently, he finished the rotis and the capsicum curry she had made for him.

"I am damn sure that this is your preparation, not Varuna's," Sid commented as he washed his hands.

"How did you guess?" Shanaya was surprised.

"How can I not identify my wife's cooking?"

"Is it that bad?"

"Don't fish for compliments, Shanaya."

She pouted as she passed him the towel to wipe his hands.

"Okay, I agree. Your rotis can fix my mood any time," he appreciated her cooking.

"Yeah." She nodded complacently.

"Where is your modesty, girl?" He laughed. She threatened to hit him.

"I have something to show you, Shanaya." He pulled her beside him as he sat on the sofa in the living room. She looked on with curiosity as he took out a rolled piece of paper from his office bag.

"No more gifts, Sid," she chided. She was tired of exchanging them.

"Not a gift. This is your reward."

She was perplexed.

He had tied the paper with a satin ribbon.

Shanaya untied the bow to read the contents of the printed sheet.

Dear Shanaya,

With reference to the proposal for *A Dash of Hope and A Dollop of Love*, we are interested in having a look at the complete manuscript. We would request you to kindly send the complete manuscript to our address for our evaluation.

Regards,
BubbleInk Publishers.

"Pinch me, Siddharth," she whispered.

He did that. "Ouch, it hurts," she complained.

"I want you to understand that you are in the world of reality, sitting on the sofa in the Saxenas' residence, reading the 'we are interested' mail from one of India's top publishers."

"But how?" Shanaya stammered.

"I was your first beta reader, Shanaya."

She gasped.

"I read through your synopsis and the initial chapters, and it left me wanting more."

Observing the disbelief on her face, he told her harshly, "Don't wear that look. You are a talented writer and all you have to do is believe in yourself. My judgement was not biased just because I—" he stopped himself just in time.

"Just because you?" she prompted, interested to know what he had been about to say.

Denying his feelings, he added, ". . . just because you are my friend. The plot was gripping and you captured my interest in the first three chapters."

"And what did you do?" She wanted to know the whole story.

He continued, "I hired a professional editor, got the blurb and the first three chapters edited. Then I sent a query letter to all the top publishing houses with a proposal, pitching it for you and requesting them to take a look."

"Oh my . . . why did you do that?"

"Because you have talent, Shanaya. But you were letting life overrule you and this was not on your priority list. You were just going with the flow of life. Your job and home came first, and you put this book on the back burner. Talent never thrives in this scenario."

What Sid said was true. Shanaya had not concentrated much on her writing since she had gotten married. Her attention was captured by something else—mostly him.

"Now you don't have time. Two more weeks . . . you have to push yourself to complete what you have started so beautifully," he instructed.

Speechless, she nodded.

"You taught me about life, Shanaya. We will grow together."

"What if they don't like my manuscript?"

"So what? Don't lose your life thinking about the what-ifs. Don't fall prey to them."

She flushed guiltily.

"And it is okay to fail, Shan. You taught me that. No one will complain. Anyway, I will be there for you, to deal with your failures and to celebrate your victories. And beware, I am a tough taskmaster . . . I will make you try again." His intense gaze captivated her.

His gesture touched her . . . moved her. She felt pampered. With tears in her eyes, she wrapped her arms around him and pulled his head towards her.

"I am really happy that you are in my life, Siddharth," the heartfelt words tumbled out of her lips. "And thank you for this start," she whispered into his ears.

"Go ahead, little bird . . . capitalise on it. Your time will come," he smiled.

"It will." She nodded.

***

Shanaya and Siddharth worked towards their respective goals the next week. And she helped him as well. Whenever her mind thought of a good one-liner, she texted him. They worked hard. In spite of the work pressure and the professional sword hanging over his head, he stayed sane because of her. They did their workouts together and had early-morning discussions to decide on important issues when their brains were hyperactive. Shanaya's workload at the office had reduced since Prashit was back. She just had to create interesting content for the newspaper to survive. To her, it was like getting paid to eat a piece of cake. The only thing that worried her was that after she moved to the content section, she was not able to see Sid as often as she would have liked to.

She left the office by five on that day and asked Varuna to prepare Sid's favourite aloo parathas for dinner. She believed that he required loads of energy to survive the gruesome ordeal. She sighed wearily. He was pushing himself so hard!

Hope he gets some time to cool off after this crisis, she prayed. With a cup of coffee, she started working on her novel. The blank pages turned into pages of emotions and feelings as the words poured out of her fingers. Her novel was based on the trauma she had faced in her childhood. Time flew, and she was riveted to the screen.

Sid walked in some time later to see Shanaya completely engrossed in her own world. She had not even noticed him entering the house. The sound of his arrival had not disturbed her. He was pretty sure that she had not eaten either.

With a plate of food in his hands, he sat in a chair next to her worktable. The scraping sound of the chair jolted her back to reality. She grimaced. "When did you come?"

He put his hands on his hips. "And I thought that with my charm I could distract you any time."

"Sid, sorry," she apologised.

He kissed her on the lips. "That is okay. It is not exactly a criminal offence."

"Wait. Let me serve you dinner." She stood up.

"Sit down." He pushed her back. "I had mine with Prashit today. I messaged you earlier. But I don't think you saw it. You were in your own zone." He smiled.

"Yeah . . . I was in the flow," she accepted guiltily.

"I brought you dinner."

His thoughtful gesture moved her. He was breaking her barriers slowly.

"Why did you?" she stammered.

"Don't break that flow, Shanaya. Go ahead with your work. I'll feed you."

Before she could resist, he fed her a mouthful of aloo paratha dipped in raita[9].

"Smells yum. I should have waited to have my dinner here instead of swallowing the dry sandwiches from the office cafeteria."

She laughed. "Serves you right. I asked Varuna to prepare these specially for you."

"Don't skip dinner, Shanaya. You come home drained and tired after a long day of work."

She nodded as he continued, "As you told me, health matters. Don't overwork yourself without food."

"Okay, boss." She saluted, wiping the traces of aloo from her lips.

"And the one-liner you sent me today was fantastic. I have found the right segment of people to target. We are starting our campaign from next Friday," he said enthusiastically.

"Great! My novel will be done by then. I can support you fully," she volunteered. The plate was empty.

He kissed her on the forehead and got up to go to bed. "I am tired, Shanaya. I am going to sleep."

---

9   An Indian yogurt-based side dish made with chopped cucumber or other vegetables and spices.

"Yes, please. Don't let me disturb you." Her concern was genuine.

Siddharth slept off and woke up again in an hour to bring her a cup of steaming coffee.

"Please don't spoil your sleep," she chided.

"That is okay. Making coffee for you will not kill me," he brushed her comment aside and passed the cup to her.

"No one has ever taken care of me this way," she murmured emotionally. She traced the contours of his face absently.

"Arre, it is just a cup of coffee. Now be a good girl. Have it and finish your writing faster. It is almost midnight."

Shanaya agreed gratefully. Sid went back to bed. When the alarm rang an hour later, Shanaya had slept too.

CHAPTER FIFTEEN

The Big Fat Misunderstanding

Beware! The world of misunderstanding creates a doomsday for any relationship, stealing trust and belief, eventually killing everything in it.

***

Shanaya and Sid tied themselves with the rope of love without any explicit declaration. Their marital bond grew with their friendship. But neither of them voiced the three little words. She convinced herself that work pressure demanded that she put her love life aside for a few days.

But it was becoming increasingly difficult for her to hide her love. She brightened up like a lamp whenever he was near her. She was done with her novel. The full manuscript had been submitted to the publishers.

It was almost eight. Darkness had settled in. Her husband was still in the office. Most of the employees had left. Humming the latest Bollywood tune, she met Prashit outside Sid's cabin. She had left for home earlier and had come back specifically to meet her husband.

"Please go ahead, Shanaya," Prashit said respectfully.

She frowned. As she was about to knock on Sid's cabin door, Prashit told her with a wink, "Why should you knock before entering your husband's cabin?"

She was flabbergasted. "How come . . ." she stammered.

"The boss told Kiran and me when we were discussing something else." He winked. "And if Kiran knows, then the whole office knows," he added.

"This was what I was afraid of. I wanted to be recognised for my work here. Not as Siddharth's wife." Shanaya was worried.

"Arre, Shanaya, you are the brain behind the one-liners. You are already in everyone's good books here," he told her honestly.

He observed her blush. "You guys make a beautiful pair and deserve each other. Please come together to meet my daughter. She keeps telling me that she wants to meet the girlfriend of her 'boss uncle'—that is what she calls our boss."

"We are planning to. Just that we are caught up with the campaign right now. Is she okay?"

"As good as any little girl can be."

That brought a smile to her lips. She went inside the cabin.

"Mr Siddharth Saxena, I will not let you continue working unless you have some food first." She pointed to the basket she was carrying, indicating that she had brought his dinner for him.

She was dressed in a yellow saree, earrings, and shoes. She had redone her make-up before meeting him again.

"You might look beautiful, my dear wife, but I am the boss here. I make the rules," he told her arrogantly. His attention went back to his laptop.

"Then break them for me." Her voice was seductive.

She knew Prashit would not allow anyone inside until she came out. Now that the secret was out, she could play her game safely. She kept the dinner basket on the chair. Gently swaying her hips, she walked towards him. "If you don't break your rules, then I'll make you break them."

With those words, she sat on the table, obstructing him from seeing his laptop. Noting her naughty look, he murmured, "Move."

"No, I will not." Though her voice was mischievous, it was stern.

"You will," he promised as he got up from his chair.

They stood close to each other as they were transported to another world where no one existed . . . no *India-Bliss,* no office troubles.

"You are a temptress," he murmured into her ears. Her cheeks burned, and she turned away, not able to withstand the romantic byplay she had started.

"No, don't." He forced her to meet his eyes. His white check shirt fluttered with the breeze coming in from the window, which was partly open.

"Do you want me to eat?"

"Yes." She nodded.

"Are you offering yourself to me as my dinner?" Sid questioned her mischievously.

Her lips trembled and she bit them nervously.

The way she stood there, awaiting his touch, mesmerised Sid. "You are beautiful, Shan!"

Passion snaked through them and the atmosphere was charged with an aura of sensuality. He smothered her forehead with feather-light kisses. But she wanted more, and her drugged eyes pleaded him. A smile lit his face at her response. With one hand, he held her shoulders, and with the other, he stroked her arms as the heat rose within her, ready to explode. Turning her slightly, he kissed her neck, and her knees buckled, unable to take it anymore. His hot breath brushed her ears, and her nerves trembled at his touch.

His mouth felt the softness of her lips. Her cupid's bow was perfectly shaped, and the arcs stood out, tantalising him and making him want to taste them.

"I am going crazy. Tell me to stop, Shanaya."

She did not respond.

"Shan, if you don't say a word, I will not be responsible for what happens next."

She moaned.

"I can't hold myself back any longer," he whispered.

But before he could finish, she pulled him to her and the words evaporated with the heat of their passion. Senseless, he claimed her lips, and their fingers were entwined in a moment of togetherness. He groaned softly, low in his throat, and then his arms pulled her closer, gathering her against him.

For this to continue further, he had to tell her that he loved her, Siddharth's brain reminded him sluggishly. She should not misinterpret his actions. His heart longed for her, and she had to be aware of his feelings towards her. There was no time better than the present. This was the moment of truth. He pushed her a little, still holding her hands as he met her gaze.

"Open your eyes, Shanaya," he murmured.

She did as he requested. Holding her gaze, he whispered, "I have to tell you something before this happens."

She watched him in anticipation. "Shanaya . . . I—"

His mobile rang right at that moment. "Damn!" he muttered. "Call from the campaign team. I have to take this. Duty calls," he murmured wistfully.

Taking his mobile, he moved to the window of his cabin. The view from there was breathtaking. There were no buildings opposite the office tower, giving them their privacy. It was an idyllic night. The stars glittered and the moonlight peeped in, as if encouraging their romance. The tall edges of the trees outside were visible, and the leaves gently rustled in the breeze.

While he finished his phone call, Shanaya sat on his chair and decided to take a look at the reports which he had been verifying earlier. She was interested in knowing how the campaign was progressing. She had planned to ask him during dinner. But instead of having dinner, they had been kissing . . .

"Oh God!" A wave of embarrassment swept through her.

Her eyes scanned the initial reports. The trial had started to work! The sales figures looked promising. She turned around to observe Sid. Deep in conversation, he had his back to her. A feeling of pride filled her. She was proud of him. This little success was a start, and he deserved more.

Ping. A message popped up on the screen of his laptop, indicating a new email. A quick glance told her who the sender was.

"Mishti Hegde."

The subject was simple: "Miss you."

Reality crashed her dreams, and she could not resist reading the email. Something prompted her to open it. Her fingers trembled as she clicked to read it.

```
My darling Sid . . .
```

"He is not your darling anymore," her heart whispered painfully to the inanimate screen as she continued reading.

```
It has been days, even months and I
have not heard your voice or seen your
smile. Do you know how hard it is for
me? Now I realise what a grave mistake
I made.
```

Shanaya clenched her fists as she willed the tension inside her to ebb away.

```
Apologies. I was not able to attend
your wedding even though you sent the
invite. Oh God! Who am I even kidding?
I did not attend your wedding because I
```

was not sure I could. I was not sure of
your parents' reaction, and I couldn't
bear to see you marrying someone else.
My heart pains even now if I think
of you with another girl. Don't get
me wrong, darling . . . I know I am
married and I am not supposed to think
this way, and I keep telling myself the
same.

"Why don't you underline that fact and put it up in your
room?" fumed Shanaya.

I attempted to stay away from you all
this time, knowing that our situations
have changed. I tried my best to move
on, but my heart struggles to listen to
my brain. My husband is a kind guy and
is wondering what he has done to me,
and I feel like the lowest form of life
for breaking his dreams, but he doesn't
know that my heart still belongs to my
Sid.

Her Sid? A wave of sadness swept through Shanaya,
making her furious over her own possessiveness.

I am stuck, Sid. I can neither move
forward nor stay behind holding onto
our treasured memories. I know that I

should have fought for you, but I did not, and I paid the price for it. I lost you. I lost my love.

"But is it my fault that I listened to my father? I don't know. Should I have become a bad daughter to prove that I was a good girlfriend? I am still a good daughter to my family. But what happened to my life? I LOST YOU, SID.

"Too late to regret, my friend," said Shanaya.

My hands are trembling as I type these words. Oh, how I wish that whatever happened in the recent past was just a bad dream . . . so that when I wake up tomorrow, I will walk into your cabin again. I can imagine it in my mind.

Shanaya turned to see her husband still talking on the phone. Her eyes went back to the screen.

Your eyes will light up on seeing me like they always did. You will drag me to your chair and kiss me, murmuring sweet nothings like you always did. And then you will propose to me with your love, making me feel like the queen of this world, and I will bask in the

```
glory of love like you did two years
back on this very day.
```

Shanaya's heart splintered into pieces. The same date . . . the same location . . . the same man. She was pretty sure that Sid had been about to propose to her minutes earlier. Did he even realise the date? Or was he trying to replace his memory of proposing to Mishti with a newer one? How cold-blooded it sounded. The more she thought about it, the more she felt bad, as if she was a substitute for someone else. She felt like an intruder between them.

```
Do you remember that day, Sid? When you
proudly told me what was inside your
heart . . . your feelings . . . your
emotions. I miss all of them. Most of
all, I miss you so much, dear. You made
me forget everything else and you still
do.
    And do you know the worst part of my
marriage? I can't let my husband near
me. I am confused. I am broken. I am so
frustrated that I want to bang my head
against the wall. I want to rip off the
clutches of my marriage and run back to
you. I want to enjoy the warmth of your
hug one more time. I know it is wrong.
Don't preach to me about morals.
    I am hurting within and I don't know
what to do. I feel sorry for the man I
```

married. I can't keep hurting him as well. I have to meet you, Sid . . . please. To see your eyes glazed with love for me . . . just one more time . . . to conclude everything once and for all. I came to Bangalore on work, and I will be here for a couple of months. Looking forward to seeing you.

Love, Mishti.

"I have to meet you," the words reverberated inside Shanaya's head. Mishti needed another chance. She stood up, and her legs wobbled as her emotions made her weak.

What did Siddharth want? Utterly confused, she watched him as he completed his call and walked back to her.

"The campaign is doing really well, Shan."

His fingers brushed hers. Angrily, she moved her hands out of his reach. Frowning, he looked at her questioningly. "What happened?"

She backed off without a reply. Her eyes were still on the laptop. With an astuteness he was always appreciated for, Siddharth quickly caught what was disturbing Shanaya.

His eyes went blank as he scrolled through the email. His clenched hands portrayed his emotions. His jaw jerked for a second in response to the email. Attuned to his every action, Shanaya took note of everything.

He is suffering, she thought. She should not fall into this emotional trap. Turning to him, she demanded, "What were you about to say earlier, Siddharth?"

He stretched his hands over his head and flopped into his chair. "Don't get this wrong, Shan," he pleaded.

"There is nothing wrong with this email, Sid. Nothing is wrong with you or with her. I am the one who has committed the sin. I feel like an intruder, breaking up the lovebirds. She has asked for another chance."

With her eyes full of angry tears, she turned away from him.

He jumped up and grabbed her arms, not letting her leave. Forcing her to meet his eyes, he muttered, "Don't do this to us, Shanaya. Let me explain."

"There is nothing to explain, Sid." She pulled her hand out of his clasp.

"You are not in the mood to listen," he said.

The tears threatened to overflow. She did not want him to see how much of an emotional wreck she was. She turned away.

Even Siddharth was broken. She could see that.

When she was at the door, he asked, "Are you okay?"

His voice halted her and she faced him again. "Don't ever use me as a replacement for Mishti."

As Shanaya stormed out, she did not notice Mayank, who entered Siddharth's cabin with a knock.

CHAPTER SIXTEEN

The Pain of Love

The belief that the one you love doesn't love you back can rip you apart. Don't give pain the power to deter you; life is all about how you deal with the scars.

***

After the fiasco at the office, Siddharth found that Shanaya was not her usual friendly self. True, she answered his queries, but she never spoke a word beyond that. He could feel her disappointment, but he did not know how to address it.

"Don't be stingy with your words. They are not going to cost you anything," he had said in frustration, and even to that, she had responded with a distant smile.

She now slept in another room and was asleep even before he reached home. Sid suspected that she was not eating properly. She seemed to have lost a little weight. A week had gone by since the start of their do-or-die campaign. They were getting a lot of new subscribers, and it was turning out to be a worthy investment. But he was unable to enjoy the success. His heart longed for a smile from his wife, which she was reluctant to give him. When he went past her desk, she lowered her head and did not meet his eyes. She was literally torturing him with her silence.

The next day, he caught her just when she was leaving the office. "Join me. I am leaving too."

Her face went blank, but she nodded, not wanting to create a scene in front of the others, especially when they seemed keen on following their activities. Silence prevailed in the car. "What happened? Are you not happy?" he asked her.

She carefully shielded her eyes, not revealing any emotions. "I am happy about your success, boss," she told him.

"I am not your boss, Shanaya," he growled. "If you call me boss one more time, then I am not going to be responsible for my actions."

For the first time since their dramatic fight, she met his eyes, which revealed his anger.

"And are you really happy with my success? I hear the words, but I don't see this happiness in your face," he came back sarcastically.

Her eyes revealed her pain. How could he ask that?

"God, sorry, I did not mean that, Shanaya. I am frustrated with your behaviour towards me."

She opened her eyes wide, showing her consternation.

With one hand on the steering wheel, he reached out to touch her head with his other hand.

She ducked down.

"Don't do this. I am not a murderer, for God's sake. What is the matter, Shanaya?"

"Nothing."

He thumped the steering wheel hard. She looked at him, hurt. Sid stopped at that, shaking his head in silence. They reached home.

"Don't forget, we have to go out," he reminded her.

She could not recall what he was talking about. Her face showed that she was clueless.

"Did you not check your email? Our campaign team has organised a dinner today to celebrate our initial success."

"Oh . . . I did not see that."

"Get ready. I am taking you."

She nodded in silence with soulless eyes.

Agitated, Siddharth walked into his room and slammed the door shut. Shanaya walked slowly to hers—the one she had used before moving into his room. After reading Mishti's email, she had moved back into her old room.

Closing the door, she heaved a sigh. Waves of depression overtook her. His concern for her killed her. But she kept telling herself that Siddharth could never be hers. If she replied to his questions, her words would reveal her pain. Sid would figure that out. That would hurt him further. She had to control herself. Falling for him had not been a part of her agenda, but she had done just that. Her heart hurt as tears flowed freely, and she did not attempt to stop them. Lifting her head, she whimpered, "Oh God! I don't know what to do. I love him so much."

She did not have time to drown in self-pity. Checking her email, she realised that they had to leave in half an hour. Splashing her face with water, she got ready in five minutes, wearing a silky blue, knee-length gown. Braiding her hair, she covered her puffed eyes with a dash of eyeliner.

Siddharth was waiting for her in the living room.

"Ready?" he enquired.

"Yes, let us go."

Observing her eyes, he asked, "Did you cry?"

Flushing guiltily, she denied, "No."

"Don't lie to me, Shanaya"

"I am not the wimpy sort," she retorted, ignoring his look.

He took hold of her hands and pleaded, "Please . . . listen to me, Shan. I did not ask Mishti to send that email."

"I know that, Sid. You are a great guy." Her sarcasm showed.

"Why are you killing me with your words?"

"To stop you from destroying me," she muttered inaudibly.

"What did you say?" he demanded.

His mobile rang just then. Cursing under his breath, he attended to the call.

"Yeah, Prashit. We are on our way."

Turning to her, he said, "People are waiting for us. Let us go."

***

Crystalz had all the elegance of a seven-star hotel. An entertainment hall in the east wing had been booked for the celebration, and a buffet dinner was arranged for the top fifty employees of *India-Bliss* who had worked tirelessly for the campaign.

As Siddharth walked in with Shanaya, the HR manager, Hari, screamed from the stage, "A hearty welcome to our CEO, Mr Siddharth Saxena, and our storyteller, Ms Shanaya Dixit, or should I say Mrs Shanaya Saxena, the lady who finally managed to drag our handsome boss into the web of matrimony?"

The crowd cheered.

"Come on, both of you," he invited them to a small stage, adorned with curtains.

"What would you like to say to your employees here, Mr Siddharth?"

"Thanks for making such excellent arrangements in so short a span of time, Hari."

"It is my job, boss," winked Hari.

Smiling at his comment, Sid addressed the crowd.

"I would sincerely like to thank each and every one of you. Without your combined efforts, we could not have had such a successful start. You guys have brought us into the safe zone and you all definitely deserve this round of applause. Here you go!"

The employees clapped for themselves as Sid did the same. "Capitalising on our start, we have to step on to the next phase. Continue working the same way, and that is not far off. I am ecstatic about the way things are progressing— so let us celebrate that this evening. I request all of you to take your mind off work tonight and have some fun. Also, please don't forget to enjoy the scrumptious dinner."

The crowd acknowledged his speech with another round of applause.

As Sid took a step back, Hari turned towards Shanaya. "And most of us never knew that you are our Mrs Boss!" The comment caused a wave of laughter amidst the employees.

Shanaya blushed. "But I have to congratulate you, Shanaya. Your one-liners were our lifesavers."

"I am a writer, Hari . . . so it was not a difficult thing for me," she brushed aside his compliment modestly.

"Wow, Mr Siddharth, you are married to a girl with beauty and creativity," he teased.

Hari turned towards the audience. "Can you all guess which one of Shanaya's one-liners worked the best?"

As the people silently waited, Hari opened a sheet of paper in his hand and read, "I am crying, but there is no one to wipe my tears. Because I am waiting for someone whom I want to claim, but I can't."

He turned to Shanaya and teased, "When our dashing CEO is here, who is that *someone*, Shanaya?"

Sid frowned. *Who is she waiting for?*

Her voice wobbled a little as she laughed to cover it up. "Arre, it was just a thought that popped into my mind."

"Yeah, you are right. We are probably reading too much into it."

"No more questions. People are waiting for dinner." Siddharth stopped Hari before he could continue.

"Don't be mean, Sid . . . just one more question. The people are interested to hear from you. What do you think of Shanaya?"

"She means a lot to me. Without her, I am nothing." He gave her a bear hug. She gasped.

"Wow, how romantic!" exclaimed Hari.

While the others present in the hall saw the love in Sid's hug, Shanaya saw it as a hug of gratitude.

"Ladies and gentlemen, let me not hold you up anymore. I can hear the sound of rumbling stomachs. Feel free to enjoy this beautiful moment with some tasty food. We deserve this success and many more to come."

The employees dispersed happily. The moment they stepped down to get their plates at the buffet, Shanaya purposely lost Sid in the crowd. Rohit joined her.

"Hey, you are a sly fox."

"Not you too!" exclaimed Shanaya.

"You kept postponing our house-hunting plans whenever our boss called you. You never told me that you are the wife of the great man himself."

"I am an employee here, just like you."

"You are not just any employee, Shanaya. Yeah, now I get our boss' jealousy that day when I was having lunch with you."

"Siddharth was not jealous," she retaliated.

"What? Of course, he was. Where are your eyes?"

Siddharth joined them after piling his plate with food.

"I am not going to intrude on your space this time." Rohit went off with a laugh.

Seeing the look of despair on Shanaya's face, Sid commented, "You can't hide behind Rohit."

"I am not."

"I believe you." His voice dripped with sarcasm.

"I booked my tickets to Delhi. I have not seen my parents for a long time."

"For how long will you be gone?"

"I don't know."

Siddharth's temper rose a notch. "Don't do this, Shanaya. You are using this trip as an excuse to avoid me."

"Meeting my parents is not a crime, Sid."

"I know that. But I will miss you," he told her frankly.

"You will have other activities to occupy yourself."

He frowned.

"Did you meet Mishti?" The words were out of her mouth before she could stop them. She did not want to sound like a jealous wife.

Until that second, Siddharth had thought that she was upset with Mishti's email. But now her query gave him some hope.

"Are you jealous?" he queried.

"Why should I be?"

"Yeah, to feel possessive towards your partner, you have to have some feeling for him, right?"

"Yes."

"And you don't feel anything for me?"

"No." And let God not strike her dead for that awful lie. She crossed her fingers behind her back.

"Or have you realised that you have feelings for someone else?" Siddharth probed intensely.

"What are you talking about?" demanded Shanaya, completely shocked by his query.

"Don't tell me that Mayank did not come to meet you," he said, sounding critical.

She fumed. When Siddharth had not elaborated on how his meeting with Mishti went, why should she talk to him about Mayank?

"Yes, I met him."

With that answer, she turned away from him.

He did not stop her. That line had hurt him.

"Oh please . . . don't fall for Mayank, Shanaya."

His eyes glittered with anger and tears.

"I will fight for you, dear. I will not let you go easily," he vowed.

As Shanaya kept her plate back, her thoughts screamed at him. *Did you really meet Mishti, Sid? Does our life not mean anything to you? Why did you not tell Mishti that she does not have a place in your life now?*

With violent thoughts burning both of them, they reached home. Shanaya went in without a word.

"Not so fast." He caught hold of her arms.

"Let go of me, Sid. I am not in the mood for your games."

"You call this a game? Seriously?"

"What else should I call it?" she shouted.

"Hah, I get it now. You treat your life with me like a game and share your love with someone else."

"Why do you keep bringing Mayank into this conversation?"

"Because he saved you and you have feelings for him?" His accusation ended in a half-query.

"There are different kinds of feelings in this world, Sid. I do feel a lot of gratitude towards him. But you have been pushing Mayank at me ever since Sakshi told you my childhood story."

"Which you should have told me in the first place."

"Not really. It is my past. Those incidents happened in my life long before I met you."

"But I told you about Mishti."

"Yes, because she is still a part of your life even after our marriage. I have a feeling that you are pushing me towards Mayank because you want to get back to Mishti."

"Stop it, Shanaya." He closed her mouth with his hands. "Get back to Mishti? Have you gone nuts? She is married, for God's sake!"

He looked into her eyes deeply. "You do believe that I will go back to Mishti."

He moved close to her in anger. "How could you?"

"No." Shanaya twisted her face. Locked against the wall, she could not move.

"You are not mine, Sid," she whispered in anguish.

He pulled out the mangalsutra around her neck.

"What does this tell you? Am I not yours?"

"Yes, legally. But morally?"

He tugged her towards him and kissed her forcibly on her lips as she struggled to get out of his embrace. As he continued kissing her, Shanaya's struggles were futile, and she started to give in to the soul-consuming feeling, more powerful than any addictive drug. Sid continued kissing her in an attempt to prove that she was all his. He tasted the saltiness of her tears.

"And you are mine. Never forget that," he whispered forcefully.

The more he kissed her, the more Shanaya wanted him. She could feel the anger and the passion in his kiss as her resistance faded. Holding his head for support, she buried her fingers into his hair. She realised that she was returning his kiss with equal fervour. Feeling ashamed of herself for giving in so quickly, she pushed him away unexpectedly.

"Don't kiss me just to cover up your feelings for your ex-girlfriend," she retaliated. The emotions that she felt were taking their toll on her. Her voice was hoarse.

"You believe that I will kiss you just to hide my feelings for Mishti?" His voice was calm, but she could feel the turbulence behind it. Frightened by his stance, she stayed silent.

"If you really believe that, then we should get a divorce."

With those words, he walked to his room. For the second time that day, he slammed the door on her face.

CHAPTER SEVENTEEN

Dreams Define You

*Don't let difficulties disturb your dreams; don't let
burdens overshadow your soul. Troubles come and go, but
dreams define you forever. Hug them tight.*

***

Shanaya's eyes were riveted on the screen. She
had not noticed Siddharth, who stood beside her.

```
Dear Shanaya,

We read through the complete
manuscript and we would be happy
to take it up for publishing.
We have a wide distribution
network, and your book will be
available throughout India. I
have attached a draft contract
with this email. Please take
```

a look at it and revert. Awaiting a
positive response from you. Wishing
you good luck in your new journey.

Regards,
Sheetal,
BubbleInk Publishers

Siddharth turned to see the happiness on her face. But all he saw was regret. But why? He was perplexed. This was her long-time dream, and there was not even a trace of a smile in her eyes. Her dull eyes were staring beyond the screen. Shanaya was about to click the delete button when he stooped forward and held her hand tightly.

"No, don't," he warned her.

She turned to him with bewildered eyes. When had he come into her room? How long had he been staring at her?

"What are you doing, Shanaya?"

"Nothing." She flushed guiltily.

"Don't lie!" he stormed.

She lowered her head and did not answer.

"Look at me." He lifted her chin with his fingers. "Why were you going to delete that email?"

"I did not," she denied.

"You would have, had I not stopped you."

Her voice quivered. "My life is a mess."

He was surprised to see her broken. He was not going to let that happen.

"So?"

"I don't care if my book gets published or not."

"Are you nuts? This is your dream coming true." He was furious.

"I don't care. If that makes me a maniac, so be it."

Sid struggled to hold on to his temper. Observing his reaction, she murmured, "You don't get it, Siddharth."

Tears rolled down her cheeks.

"I understand more than you think I do. Why do you let your agony disturb the dreams that you hold dear?"

She murmured, "Probably because I put my personal life before my dreams."

"Life and dreams are intertwined. Don't try to separate them," he chided her.

Seeing her teary face, he added grimly, "Don't make the same mistake that I made, Shanaya. Don't let your feelings disturb your career and dreams. Don't let day-to-day happenings spoil your goals. It is highly difficult to get these opportunities again."

He was right. But her feelings for Siddharth dominated her mind and she did not want to try anything else. She broke down. Her hands covered her face.

With a muttered curse, he came forward and held her hands supportively. "Don't do this to yourself, Shan. Whatever happens in your personal life, don't let it ruin your hopes and drag you down. Keep going. One day, things will get back into perspective."

He came closer to her ears and whispered to her the same way she had done a long time back. "Your time will come!"

Those magical words made the impact, and she launched herself at him. Siddharth ruffled her hair gently as her sobs slowed down. Their souls melted into one in a simple hug.

"Relax, Shanaya." He held her face with both his hands and realised that she was burning.

"Oh my God, Shan! You have fever!" he exclaimed.

"No," she denied. He touched her forehead to confirm it.

"Yes." With that affirmation, he carried her and gently laid her on her bed. Then he covered her with a duvet.

"I will call the doctor," he informed her.

Shanaya felt too weak to stop him from taking over. She was overwrought by emotions and her head pounded with pain. She slept off.

Her eyes half opened a little later when she heard the doctor declare, "She is just stressed. Seems like the common flu. Let her rest it out. I will give her some sedatives so that she can sleep peacefully."

"Thanks, doc," Siddharth replied as he walked out with the doctor to get the medicines.

He came back with a cup of steaming coffee and some bread.

"A cure for your headache, Shanaya. Have it."

"Am feeling guilty, Sid."

"For what?"

"For making you do all this."

"You did not do it on purpose, right? Or did you? Oh God, Shanaya . . . you are overworked . . . and you were not ready to delegate the household work either," he criticised her.

"I cooked because I wanted to. I have always loved seeing you enjoy my food. It is my guilty pleasure," she declared weakly.

He shook his head at her stubbornness.

"Look at what it has led to."

He put his finger on her lips to stop her from arguing.

"Have these tablets and then rest."

She pushed his hand away. "You are a tyrant, Sid. How am I supposed to take them with your finger on my lips?"

With a half-hearted laugh, he removed his hand.

She took the medicine and went to sleep serenely.

Careful not to disturb her, Siddharth slept by her side on the couch. She might need him during the night.

Two days passed. It made him happy to fuss around her like a mother hen. He slept with that thought lingering in his mind.

Shanaya screamed exactly when the clock hit twelve that night. "What the hell?" Siddharth rushed to her.

"Mayank!" Her voice was shrill.

He froze at her words.

Is she dreaming about him?

She screamed again in horror. "No, please . . . let Mayank stay."

Her words killed him.

"Shanaya, wake up."

He rocked her out of her nightmare.

She opened her eyes to see Sid half bent over her. He switched on the lights. She was sweating profusely.

"Are you all right, Shanaya?" he asked her, visibly shaken.

She nodded. "I had some bad dreams. My past took over," she whispered.

He got her a glass of water from the kitchen.

"Calm down. Are you okay?"

"I am feeling all right, Sid. Please, let us go back to sleep." With disturbed thoughts crowding his mind, he covered her with her quilt again as she tried to sleep.

He let out a sigh. Shanaya still dreamt about Mayank. She had met him again. That thought made his heart bleed. He tossed and turned restlessly, unable to sleep.

***

The rays of the morning sun hit Shanaya through the curtains of her balcony. She felt fresh after two days of recuperation. Taking the days off, Siddharth had fussed over her, and she felt relaxed after a long time. She smiled. She was starting to believe that Sid really loved her. Elated at the thought, she got up and went to the kitchen.

```
Leaving for office today. Got you some
sandwiches. Not my preparation, though.
You should thank Varuna later.
```

The sandwiches were wrapped in aluminium foil. Even if Varuna had prepared them, Shanaya's gut feeling told her that Sid had wrapped them up to keep them fresh. Varuna normally placed the sandwiches in a closed container. She smiled at his thoughtful gesture. She crossed over to the drawing room and was surprised to see that the door to Sid's studio room was partly open.

She smiled. After she had asked him to continue painting, she had not gone inside. But curiosity got the better of her today.

She walked in and was stunned at what she saw. Her heart was racing, and she felt giddy looking at the new painting that Siddharth had made. The smell of fresh paint was overpowering. There was no trace of Mishti in the room.

She touched the edges of the window-sized painting hanging in the centre of the wall. It was still wet. He must have completed it recently, probably yesterday, she guessed.

Staring back at her from the canvas were her own bright brown eyes. Sid had captured the moment they had stood near the bike under the rain. She was laughing, and Sid was gazing at her intently. The look in his eyes was almost convincing. Did he love her as she did?

Truly, madly, deeply? The only hurdle she had now was the Mishti factor. Even if Sid had feelings for her, would his heart change if he saw Mishti again in his life? How could she trust him?

***

Shanaya went to the office later that day. It was buzzing with activity. Everyone seemed to be in a joyous mood. The gloomy atmosphere was gone. But what really caught her eyes were the huge televisions put up throughout the office, showing visuals of Siddharth along with some stats.

Rohit walked towards her. "You are back after your sick leave. Are you all right, Shanaya?" he asked with concern.

"I am fine." She smiled back. Noting her looking at the TV screen, he commented, "The big boss has done it. Our campaigns were a huge success. The papers that had printed that we would be sinking soon, are all praises for our proactive approach. Investors are now showing a lot of interest in us. We are back in business with a bang. Mr Siddharth has done it, Shanaya!" he declared proudly.

Shanaya's heart soared as people around her praised Sid. Her attention went back to the screen. The news reporter invited Siddharth for an interview. In his white T-shirt and blue jeans, Sid looked informal but gorgeous.

"*India-Bliss* magazine has managed to triumph amidst the adversities that were pulling it down in this digital world. Meet the young and dashing CEO of *India-Bliss*, who led the way for the magazine," the reporter welcomed him.

"Hello, Priyanka!" smiled Siddharth.

"So, to whom do you attribute this mind-blowing success, Mr Siddharth Saxena? *India-Bliss* is back with a bang. The sales numbers are soaring as per recent reports."

"My determined employees. They worked hard day and night to achieve this. Thanks, guys!" He raised his hand in acknowledgement.

The crowd in the office cheered and whistled.

"He is a good leader," someone claimed.

Shanaya was overwhelmed. To hear that the person you love is responsible for all this success was a sweet feeling, and she was thoroughly enjoying it.

"That is a nice thing to say," remarked the reporter.

"It is the truth. This success is all because of their smart work."

"I understand that, Mr Siddharth, but as the person at the helm, you have to drive things right. I think you are too modest!" She laughed.

"Yeah, I took the lead on this campaign, but there was someone else who helped me throughout. She stood by me through my failures and kept pushing me."

"She?" the reporter pried.

"Ha ha. Yes, it is definitely a 'she' . . . in fact, a beautiful 'she'. The one who drove me until I reached my destination is my better half, my life partner, my love, Mrs Shanaya Saxena."

The entire office clapped. Shanaya's eyes clouded with emotional tears. Sid had declared her as his love. A shot of elation gripped her soul. The whistles and claps sounded far away. The buzz around her seemed distant.

"Awesome, Shanaya!" congratulated Rohit.

"He is proud of you, Shanaya. You deserve it," Prashit joined them. People crowded around her. She struggled to control her emotions. This was a recorded program. Had Sid come back to the office? She wanted to rush inside and meet him. She wanted to demand to know if he truly loved her, or was it just for publicity?

"Where is Mr Siddharth, Prashit?" she asked his PA.

They moved away from the crowd and stood outside his empty cabin.

"He has not returned from the TV station."

"Oh, I did not know that!" she exclaimed.

"I met him this morning before he left for the show. And he came on his bike."

"Bike?" She was confused. Why did Sid take his bike and not his car? Where was he now?

"Oh, Sid, please come back soon. I am so happy for you, and I can't wait to meet you," she murmured to herself.

She called his mobile. There was no response. She frowned. Why was he not picking up her calls?

Her face revealed her distress.

"Don't worry. He will be back soon. He can't stay away from you for long," Prashit teased her.

"Not just our boss. This lady has also fallen hard for her husband," Rohit added laughingly into the conversation.

Did it appear that way? Shanaya wondered. Did they look like a couple of lovebirds to the onlookers?

She blushed. *Where is he?*

Her pathetic mind wanted a confirmation of his love, or to be precise, she wanted him to say, "I love you and only you . . . not Mishti anymore." The words kept ringing in her ears as she waited for him.

CHAPTER EIGHTEEN

The Chase

Reciting the "I love you" mantra doesn't mean that someone loves you for real. Don't fall for words. What really matters is how much they value you.

***

From the TV station, Siddharth started on his way back, but he did not want to get back to the office just yet. His professional work was done, but what weighed him down was Shanaya's dream last night.

She had called out for Mayank in her sleep and that irked him. Did that mean that she loved Mayank still? And here he had declared proudly to the world that he loved her.

What an emotional idiot I am! He cursed himself.

Was he always doomed when he loved someone?

Subconsciously, he noticed that he was on the same road that he had travelled on with Shanaya the day they had gone to Raghu's office. He checked his watch—it was only three in the afternoon, but the darkened clouds and the chilly weather created the illusion that it was past six in the evening. He stopped at the chocolate sandwich shop.

"Bhaiya, could you please pack a couple of chocolate sandwiches?" he asked.

"Sure, sir." The shopkeeper peered at him as he recognised him. "Did your girlfriend not come with you?"

"No, and she is my wife," Sid corrected him.

"Wife? But you were not fighting. In fact, you guys were enjoying yourselves, and I assumed . . ." he faltered.

Sid smiled mildly. "That is okay. Everything is the same to me. The tags might be different—girlfriend or wife—but I will always love her."

He cursed himself again. What was he doing? Not content with declaring his love to the world, he was now talking about his feelings with a shopkeeper.

"Oh God," he murmured.

Giving him the parcel, the shopkeeper observed the love in his eyes. "Give my regards to *didi*[10]. Tell her she is lucky to have you."

"You are wrong, bhaiya. I am lucky to have her. But I am not sure if I am lucky enough to keep her for life." On that note, he left with his sandwiches.

---

10 Hindi word for an older sister.

Shanaya was not with him, yet Sid could feel her holding him from behind.

"I have gone mad," he muttered as he started his bike. She appeared to have blended into his life. His turbulent emotions engulfed him. The wind made his eyes water, and he could taste his tears. He stepped up the speed by a notch and rode around aimlessly. The main road disappeared from his sight. His vision was clouded with the wetness of his misery, and he could not take it anymore. He slowed down and stopped his bike at the corner of a deserted road which was lined with trees on both sides. It was misty and the visibility was low. There was not a soul in sight. Under normal circumstances, he would have described the environment around him as being eerie, but right now it did not matter to him. The dark clouds and the harsh cries of the birds made zero impact on him. It seemed like a perfect spot for introspection.

He sat on a rock with his head in his hands. He had stayed calm for far too long. He unleashed the emotions that were bottled up inside him. His sobs broke out loud and clear. Somewhere, his mind reminded him that men are not supposed to cry. He pushed the thought away. He was human after all, and a love-struck human at that. Tears ran down his face with no one to stop him from crying. He stood up in frustration.

"I can't take this anymore."

He screamed into the woods at the top of his voice. The cold wind whooshed around him. Dead leaves fluttered everywhere.

"Shanaya, I need you. I can't give you up."

He heaved a sigh. Mayank had come to visit him at the office that day. Introducing himself as her friend, he had asked for Shanaya. Instead of confronting him, Sid had acted like a gentleman and told him where to meet her, controlling his monstrous feelings of jealousy. Because he knew that whatever his feelings might, he could not decide things for Shanaya. She had to make her choice. The decision had to come out of her own free will.

"Mayank might be a good fellow. He may have saved you, but still . . ."

He hit his wrist on the rock. "Damn!"

"You are mine, Shanaya . . . my wife. You taught me what is love. And I love you."

A sense of peace engulfed him as he admitted his love wholeheartedly. As if Mother Nature wanted to lend her support, the wind slowed down. The evening sun peeped out from behind the clouds. Sid sat down again with a sigh and closed his eyes. He wandered into the world of his own thoughts, where his brain began convincing his heart.

"People in love are not selfish, Sid. If Shanaya loves Mayank, you have to let her go."

"But Shanaya was the one who taught me to fight for love," his heart countered.

"Yes, when both people are in love . . . but that is not the case here," his brain argued back.

"Does she not love me then?"

"Better check with her," the rational inner voice suggested.

"But what if she loves Mayank and your question puts

her in an embarrassing situation and she pities you?" his heart questioned.

He shook his head. "I don't want her pity." Decision made, he looked at the sky. It was almost seven in the evening. She could be looking for him, and the sandwiches would go bad soon.

He had to let her go. But if she gave him even one sign that she loved him, he would hold on to her for the rest of his life. The thought finally put a smile on his lips, and he started back home.

He saw her as he crossed the sandwich shop again.

"Shanaya!" he called out.

Her heart leapt when she saw him.

She ran to him. "Where have you been, Sid? Are you okay? We were all worried. After your interview, we were not sure where you had gone. I even wanted to report you as missing to the police. But Prashit stopped me, asking me to wait till tonight."

"Arre, am not a kid. Don't worry." He admonished her.

He wrinkled his eyebrows. "Don't bother ordering the sandwiches. I already got them packed."

"I wanted to get you something to celebrate your success with the magazine," she told him wistfully.

"You are what I love and need," his heart murmured wordlessly, thrilled by her thoughtful gesture.

The shopkeeper waved at them, happy that they were back together.

"It does not matter. Let us go. It is getting dark," he warned. "How did you come here?" he asked her.

"Hired an autorickshaw," she replied.

He shook his head. "How many times have I told you to take the car? You should have called Ravi."

"In an auto, I could keep an eye on both sides of the road to look out for you," she told him seriously. Her concern for him undid him. She looked stunning in her yellow kurta, bordered with silk lace.

Grabbing her hand, he took her to his bike. Holding his shoulders for support, she got on the pillion seat.

"Shall we go home?" he asked her.

"If you have some time, could you please take me for a ride before we go back?" She leaned over to look at his face.

He turned around to reply. "Why not? It is not as if someone is waiting for us at home."

For almost half an hour, they kept driving down the deserted road. Shanaya desperately wanted to ask him if what he had said on TV was true.

But Sid was not in a talkative mood, and he seemed content to take in the fresh air and enjoy the pleasure of the ride.

Darkness fell gradually. Pulling up all her courage, Shanaya tapped him on his shoulder. "Siddharth."

He nodded in acknowledgement.

"Could you please stop? I need to check something with you. It is urgent."

He parked his bike at exactly the same spot where he had parked earlier—his spot.

They got off the bike, but he was a little reluctant to talk. What if she asked for a divorce? She turned away from him, towards the trees. She pulled at her kurta restlessly. Her demeanour made him anxious. "What is all the suspense about, Shanaya?"

"Sid," she swallowed her words as she turned to him.

"Did you . . ."

"Did I . . . what?"

"Did you really mean what you said on TV?"

"I spoke about a lot of issues, Shanaya . . . be more specific," he chided her even though he knew what she was referring to.

She came closer. "Do you really love me, Sid?" There, she asked the question! She heaved a sigh of relief.

"Do you?" he asked her back. Their eyes met.

"Ahh, someone, please help!" a child's voice came out of nowhere, interrupting the moment. They heard the rustle of leaves nearby.

"Someone is in trouble," Siddharth remarked, immediately becoming alert.

"Sounded like a little girl, Sid," confirmed Shanaya.

He ran to the other side of the road to check from where the voice had come. Shanaya followed him. The trees were dense, and the dry leaves crunched under their feet.

"Anyone here?" shouted Siddharth.

"Yes!" a feeble voice replied.

They moved closer towards the sound. There, they saw a little girl, about seven or eight years old. Her foot was caught in the thick roots of a wild plant and she was anxiously trying to pull it free.

"What are you doing here?" demanded Siddharth.

"You are not one of them, are you?" The girl started to cry.

He sensed that something was wrong.

"Calm down, *chotu*[11], I am not going to hurt you."

Shanaya released the girl's leg from the tangled roots.

"Thanks. I have to go, or they will catch me again," she told them.

"Who?" Sid asked again, keeping his voice patient. With her leg now free, the little girl looked at them hopefully.

"Uncle, can you help me, please?"

"You have to tell us what happened, chotu. If you don't, then how can we help you?"

"Uncle, I came with my parents to a fair nearby. But I lost them in the crowd and was searching for them when another uncle came to me and told me that he would take me to my parents. But he took me somewhere else. I refused to go with him when I realised that he was taking me somewhere else and then he hit me."

She pointed to a red mark near her lips.

Shanaya cried. It was the same story all over again. Her hands shivered as she relived her past. Siddharth feared that she was about to pass out.

"Relax." He squeezed Shanaya's hands. Bending down, he took the hands of the little girl in his, reassuring her. "Don't worry, chotu, we will help you. What happened after that?"

"There were a lot of kids there. Most of them were crying. I was there for some days. Somehow, I managed to escape today when that bulky man came to take us to another place. But he saw me, Uncle, and he began to chase me. I ran from him. He kept chasing me. I took different

---

11   Hindi word meaning little one.

turns, and then I lost him. But my leg got stuck in the roots of this tree," she cried.

"Don't worry, chotu, we will take you back to your parents," volunteered Shanaya. "Come," she invited the little girl as they walked back to Sid's bike.

"The police station might be a better option, Shan. They can help us find her parents, and they will figure out a way to help the other kids."

Though she reassured the kid, Shanaya seemed lost in her thoughts. "Shanaya." He called her again.

"My name is Shanaya too, Uncle," the little girl volunteered.

Siddharth shivered. He visualised his wife suffering as a little girl and imagined her plight. How brave she had been. He kissed her forehead gently. "Don't worry, Shan. We will make sure this little Shanaya is back safely with her parents."

She nodded as they took the child to the nearby police station. After finishing all the formalities and ensuring that the little girl's parents were on their way to pick her up, they left. The police had also confirmed that they had definite leads which would help them bring back the other children who were trapped. Shanaya waved at the girl. Happy with their work, Siddharth smiled tiredly. It was almost eleven.

"It was a traumatic experience for the little girl. I will have a word with her. It will not take much time," Shanaya told him.

"Fine. I will go and wait for you near the bike." He nodded.

Sid felt ecstatic. It was as if he had had a chance to help Shanaya herself. He did not notice the guy hovering nearby, dressed suspiciously in all black.

The moment he stepped out of the police station, someone hit him with a big iron rod from the back, right on his head.

"This is what you get for spoiling our plan," the man in black murmured venomously.

Blood splattered all over, and Shanaya screamed, running back towards Sid. The man tried to scamper away even as the police circled him.

"Sid!" she cried.

He collapsed on the ground.

CHAPTER NINETEEN

The Beginning

With delightful rays of hope, a new dawn brings a new day, yet another meaningful journey, and a new beginning to everything. It is time to move on with a smile.

***

The horrific scene unfolded right in front of Shanaya. Blood oozed out of Sid's head. She rushed to him with a heart-rending cry. A red stain spread across his white T-shirt. His body turned cold.

"Siddharth!" she called him. He wriggled a little.

"He is losing blood. Can somebody help him?" she yelled.

He struggled to open his eyes. "Stay awake, Sid!" she screamed in fear.

"Shan . . . I . . ." his voice was hoarse as his eyes shut again.

"No, please don't leave me!" She held his hands tightly. But his hands were frighteningly cold.

"Hold on, Sid . . . don't give up. I am here for you."

There was no response. "Please call an ambulance!" she shouted anxiously. The policemen had already done that. Their guilt was twofold as the incident had happened in front of the police station and Siddharth was a well-known figure in society.

Shanaya put her face on Sid's chest in order to feel his heartbeat, and heaved a sigh of relief.

"He is breathing. Don't move him," the inspector told her from behind.

"But he is unconscious," she retorted, losing her cool. Things were spinning out of her control. She closed her eyes in despair. Tears fell from her eyes even in her state of fear. She sobbed hard as the spear of sorrow pierced her.

The inspector hoped that the ambulance would arrive soon. The situation was becoming worse.

Shanaya touched Sid's pale cheeks with trembling fingers "Sid, please listen. I love you so much . . . no matter what, I will always love you. I can't imagine life without you. Please, come back."

Even the policemen got misty-eyed as they saw the plight of the young wife, who was fighting for her husband's life.

"Where is the ambulance?" Shanaya demanded again, turning to them.

"On the way, ma'am. Don't worry. He will be all right."

Her lips trembled as she looked at Sid's face, which had taken on an unhealthy pallor. It appeared that she was unlucky in love. Just when she had thought they could begin again, she seemed to have lost everything.

Lost? She crumbled again at the direction of her thoughts.

"Calm down," she murmured to herself. She knew she was panicking.

Why am I thinking negatively? Stay strong for both of us, Shanaya, she instructed herself, clenching her fists. Seconds ticked away, with each second feeling interminably long.

"Oh God, please don't take him from me," she prayed fervently. The siren of the ambulance came as the answer to her prayers.

A couple of paramedics jumped out of the ambulance, and things happened quickly after that. They put Sid on the stretcher and lifted him into the vehicle. Shanaya joined him.

Holding his hands, she kept whispering into his ears, "I love you, Sid."

She did not notice his body jerking.

***

It was almost dawn. Shanaya was tired, but she did not want to leave Sid's side. The moment they had reached the hospital, the chief doctor, Dr Shiv, had taken charge. Luckily, he had been on night duty, and things were brought under control almost immediately. The initial scans were done, and she sighed with relief when they told her that there were no serious internal injuries. The slash was deep, and needed stitches, and to top it all, Sid had lost a lot of blood. There were no clots, though.

They had moved him back to a private ward after his treatment and decided to keep him under observation, just to be on the safe side. But Shanaya had not spoken to the doctor yet. To see a strong man like Sid lying on a hospital bed broke her heart. She walked over to him and traced his fingers gently. An IV drip ran into his arm. With his bandaged head, he looked more like a handsome pirate than a patient. The doctor cleared his throat from behind.

She turned towards him.

"Mrs Saxena. He is all right. Your husband is a strong man," he began on a positive note.

"Thanks, doc," she glowed at the doctor's words.

"We have stitched the wound and sedated him. So, it will be a while before he wakes up, but don't worry. Just let him rest for a week. He will be perfectly all right and walking in no time."

She wanted to scream with joy. Her eyes glittered gratefully.

"You can go home now. Our night-duty nurse is on her rounds. You can rely on her. If there is any development, we will call you immediately," he added.

"That is okay, doctor. I will stay." Seeing his expression, she added, "I want to . . ."

Noting her determined look, the doctor smiled and left. Shanaya called Sita Aunty and informed her of the situation. She was glad that the worst had passed. "Don't panic, Aunty. Sid is going to be perfectly okay. The doctor confirmed that," she reassured her.

"But, Shanaya—"

"I will take care of him, Aunty. Don't worry. No point travelling back and forth."

"I know. But do call me if you require any help. Good night, Shanaya. Take care of my son."

After promising that she would do so, Shanaya disconnected the call and sent a message to Prashit to let him know what had happened.

Siddharth's eyes flickered open hours later. He saw her sleeping on the chair, close to his bed.

"Shanaya," he croaked.

His voice woke her up immediately. She responded with a smile, glad to see him awake

"Wah, your smile can cure any sick man," he murmured playfully.

"Are you okay?" she demanded, ignoring his attempt to joke.

"Yeah, a lot better," he declared and tried to sit up.

"No, don't. You are supposed to be on bed rest for a week," she instructed him forcefully. She tried to gently push him back on the bed.

"Shanaya," he whined. A nurse in her late fifties walked into the room to do her morning check-up.

"Hah, good . . . this boy is awake!" she exclaimed.

"Boy?" Siddharth pouted.

"Lie back. Don't move," she ordered him.

"You are right, Sister. He tried to get up," Shanaya complained.

"Bad boy. Obey your wife! Wives are always right. Anyway, how are you feeling?"

"Shouldn't that be your first query?" Sid asked her wryly.

"If you dictate what I should ask, I will chuck you out," she threatened him.

"Please do that," he countered.

The atmosphere had lightened with the nurse's arrival.

"If that is what you want, I will make you stay here for two weeks instead of one."

The ladies laughed. Completing her routine check-up, the nurse went off, looking satisfied. Shanaya looked happy. "I am reassured. She can handle you." She poked his stomach gently with her fingers.

He held her hands tightly.

"Can she handle me better than you?" he asked her with curiosity.

She nodded.

"No, I don't agree," he argued.

"Sid." She tugged her hands away as her heart fluttered at his touch.

"Do you remember what we were talking about when all this happened?"

She nodded, unable to meet his eyes.

"You did not reply," he complained.

"Neither did you."

But her heart longed for his answer. The moment was lost again, however, as Prashit entered the room just then.

"I saw the message in the morning, and I rushed here right away. Are you all right, boss?" he demanded.

"Yeah, as well as you can see," answered Siddharth, touched by his concern. He released his hold on Shanaya reluctantly.

Prashit passed a flask of coffee and a bag of fruits to Shanaya. "How did you get in? These are not visiting hours," Shanaya asked, sorry that her moment had been disturbed once again.

"I have my ways!" Prashit exaggerated. "How could I stay away after I heard that my boss was hit on the head? I rushed over, but what do I see? Instead of the doctor checking him up, he was romancing his beautiful wife!" He winked.

Shanaya blushed. But Sid was not embarrassed even a little. "And you decided to break the romance," he added in a playful tone.

Prashit laughed.

"We have still not met Nitika after she came home from the hospital," Sid told him.

"Don't worry, boss. She asked me to give you her love, and she said that she will arrange a party for you once you are out of the hospital," replied Prashit.

"Such a sweet girl. We will be there for her party," promised Shanaya.

"Agreed. Now back to business. We have a meeting with the next set of investors today, right?" Sid asked him.

"Yes, boss, but . . ."

Sid frowned at his reply.

"No," intruded Shanaya. "The doctor has advised you a week of rest, and you are not going anywhere," she told Sid.

"Did you forget that I am your boss?" demanded her husband.

"I don't care. Throw me out of your company, but you still have to stay here," she retorted.

"Boss, she is right. Let me bring your laptop to the hospital. You can handle things from here for a week. If required, I will arrange for a conference call today. I can handle things if Shanaya can share the load a little," Prashit suggested.

Siddharth's eyes were tired. He looked exhausted with all the blood loss. Shanaya stood with her hands on her hips, as if daring him to disobey the doctor's orders.

"Okay, I give up," he told them.

"Bring Sid's laptop. And I will help you," Shanaya promised Prashit.

Siddharth slowly recovered from his injuries. Things got better for *India-Bliss* as they finalised the deals with the new investors.

Shanaya and Sid worked in perfect sync from the hospital. He dictated, and she typed his emails. Prashit took care of things at the office. Shanaya represented Sid in the meetings. Things went smoothly. But one issue was burning in both their minds. They had not spoken about their love after that email from Mishti.

And Shanaya needed to know the answer to the question that was literally killing her: even if Sid loved her, what would happen if he met Mishti in person? After all, he had been ready to give his life for her once, and now Mishti was showing an interest in him again. Did his heart long for her? How could anyone forget their first love? Was it even possible? She did not know.

But Shanaya knew one thing for certain in her heart. She would not stand in their way if that was the case. She looked at Sid longingly. He caught her glance.

She blushed. Caught in the world of business, Siddharth asked her, "What are you waiting for? Send the email to Raj."

That gave her an idea. She had access to his laptop. She scrolled down through his inbox to see Mishti's email. Siddharth had not responded it.

Why not? She frowned. She turned to him and saw that he was on an official call again.

Before she could chicken out, she quickly drafted a reply to Mishti's email. She played the role of an imposter. Yet she was okay with it as she strongly believed that all was fair in love and war. And it was time to declare war.

```
Dear Mishti,

Lovely to see your email after such a
long time. I missed you too. Let us
catch up to discuss things. Meet me at
Rockton Cafe Day tomorrow at nine in
the morning. You will find my new number
at the end of this email. Message me
once you reach the place. I will be
there in five minutes.

Sid,
98XXXXXXXXX
```

Shanaya hit the send button. The deed was done. She had given Sid a chance to decide things once and for all. She wanted to know his decision, even if it hurt her.

"Have you sent it?" Siddharth turned to her. He was done with his call.

"What?" she stammered.

"The email to Raj?" he reminded her.

"Yeah." She nodded abstractedly.

"Everything is good then."

"Yes."

"Why are you replying in monosyllables? You can talk in sentences too," he retorted lightly.

How could she tell him that it was her guilt that was stopping her from talking to him?

He got up from his bed. "I am happy that I am getting discharged tomorrow. They will remove my bandages tonight. Good riddance. And . . ."

He pulled Shanaya to him. "We need to talk properly, Shanaya. I can't discuss our personal issues here in the hospital. These white and green walls disgust me."

"We will do that tomorrow. But I will go home tonight once they remove your bandages. I have to set some things before you come home."

"Yes, please do. I desperately want to taste your rotis, not Varuna's. Could you make them for me, please?"

"Deal." She put her hands in his.

***

His check-ups were all done. Dressed casually in a pair of grey jeans and a white and red striped T-shirt, Sid stepped out of the hospital. After the much-needed rest, he felt great. And today, he would tell Shanaya what was in his heart. He had a surprise for her. He knew that she loved him. He had been half-conscious when they were in the ambulance on their way to the hospital, and he had caught her declaration of love. His heart lit up as he recollected her words.

He looked at the clouds in sky, covering up the sun. The weather was not that great. Rain threatened to pour any moment now. And it was barely nine in the morning. But rain would not stop him today. His high-quality jerkin, a beautiful gift from his mother, could handle both the rain and the chilly weather.

His mobile rang just then. The call was from an unknown number.

"Hello."

He froze. It was Mishti's voice. They had deleted each other's numbers purposely so that they could move on.

"Yes."

"Mishti here," she whispered.

His mind went blank. After a couple of seconds, he answered, "Tell me." He was disturbed. He was hearing her voice after a long time.

"I am waiting for you at the Rockton Cafe Day. Join me." She disconnected the call.

Mishti was waiting for him after all this time. Was it fate? How could he avoid her? What would he say to her? He shivered a little despite his jerkin.

The driver signalled him as he brought his car to the front entrance of the hospital. "You wait here, Ram. I will be back in half an hour. I am going to the Rockton Cafe Day nearby," he told him.

"Okay, sir." He nodded.

***

Shanaya's heart fluttered. Today she would find out if Sid had moved on or not. She knew that just by looking at his face, she would get her answer. And she planned to do that by staying a couple of tables away from where Sid and Mishti would sit. She had asked their driver to drop her at the cafe before picking Sid up. She had chosen this cafe as its location was perfect for her plans—it was close to the hospital and was located in a small, secluded road with not many people around at this time of the day. People called it the lovers' cafe.

Her thoughts circled around Sid, and unaware of where she was going, Shanaya collided straight into Mishti, who stood at the front entrance of the cafe.

"Oh God," Shanaya gulped as she met Mishti's beautiful eyes. Her knee-length bluish gown was pretty.

I am going to lose my Sid to her.

"Sorry," she muttered.

"That is okay," Mishti replied.

Even her voice is sweet, Shanaya thought. She was about to step into the cafe when Mishti caught hold of her. She was astonished.

Did Mishti know her? Had Sid sent any of her pictures to her? If Mishti recognised her, then her whole plan would go for a toss. Her make-up was minimal, and she was wearing a traditional yellow kurta with black leggings.

"Have we met before?" Mishti asked her.

"No," denied Shanaya vehemently. She wanted to get in before Siddharth arrived at the cafe.

"But I have a feeling that I have seen you somewhere."

Mishti held her hands and looked at her keenly. She had some time to spare before Sid's arrival.

"Probably someone like me, but I am sure that if I had met you earlier, I would remember it," Shanaya covered up.

Mishti gasped. She recognised her now. Sid had sent her his wedding pictures, and this was Siddharth's wife. And she was pretty with an air of innocence around her.

"You are Shanaya, right?"

***

Siddharth stopped a few feet away. Standing in front of the cafe was Mishti, holding Shanaya's hands. He was perplexed.

To add to his troubles, it started to drizzle. The gloomy weather made the situation utterly pathetic. He looked up at the sky. "Oh God, give me a break," he murmured.

But seeing them together cleared his clouded thoughts. The street was silent, except for a couple of people who rushed inside the cafe to take shelter from the rain.

His arrival caught Shanaya and Mishti's attention as they stood stunned. The rain drenched them. They shivered, yet their eyes were glued to him. They did not move, but watched him like a hawk instead. It was a small road, but it seemed long as he walked slowly towards them. His heart led the way.

Shanaya's heart skidded multiple times. She would know now.

Sid removed his jerkin as he got closer to them.

"Hi, Mishti," he said and passed his jerkin to her so that she could shield herself from the pouring rain. "Why don't you go inside the cafe?" he suggested.

Mishti smiled, but she did not move. He smiled back.

Shanaya had her answer. Their smiles spoke volumes. No more doubts. Siddharth still loved Mishti. She knew it. She did not have to wait any longer. Her soul hurt. She had to give them their space.

She took a step back and tried to move away. But Siddharth clutched her hand tightly, not letting her go.

"No, don't go."

Pulling her towards him, he hugged her, covering and shielding her from the rain with his body. She looked into his eyes, confused.

"You told me that my time would come, and yes, it has . . . I have everything a man could want in this world—a successful career, and a wife I love . . ."

Shanaya gasped.

Wordlessly, Mishti walked away, throwing his jerkin aside. Neither of them stopped her. They watched her until she disappeared from their view. Sid went down on his knee, holding Shanaya's hand.

"My beautiful Shanaya, I was about to tell you today. You asked me if I love you."

He paused and looked into her eyes. "The answer is a big YES. I love you more than anything else in this world.

Everything I told the interviewer was straight from my heart, and it was nothing but the truth."

Shanaya was stunned by his confession. The rain slowed down to a drizzle. Sid got up and hugged her tightly, as if he never wanted to let her go.

A wave of ecstasy enveloped her. It was happening for real. And not in her dreams.

"You once told me that for any mistake I make, if I ask you to forgive me under the rain, you will. And so, I ask you to forgive me, Shan . . . forgive me for how I have hurt you all along. I am sorry. You are everything to me. Could you accept all my shortcomings and move on? Shall we begin again?"

"Yes, please." Shanaya nodded with tears of happiness brimming in her eyes.

Sid took out a box from his pocket. Shanaya was overwhelmed with his love. Was he going to gift her a ring? Surprised, she peered into the box.

"Oh God . . . not this," she whispered.

Nestled in a velvet bed was a beautiful red ChocoHeart—the heart she had demanded from her father years ago.

"You remembered," she whispered, her voice revealing her awe.

"Yeah." He nodded with joy. She hugged him back with all her love. "I love you, Sid . . . you don't know how much!" she exclaimed.

"I know."

She turned to him, surprised. "I could hear you partly

when we were on our way to the hospital. I thought I was hallucinating," he told her.

She smiled. "Don't make that mistake ever. My love for you is real. And I will tell you again and again for the rest of our lives. I love you, Sid."

He lifted her in his arms. She laughed and cried at the same time.

"Truly, madly, and deeply, just as I do?" he asked.

"Yes," confirmed Shanaya.

"Okay then, let us go home. We have to get ready for your book launch."

"What are you talking about?" queried Shanaya.

"Yes, I followed up with the publishers. That was the surprise that I arranged for you. Don't keep talking. You don't have much time. Let us move."

Ram drove the love-struck couple back to their home.

"I still can't believe this," Sid commented as he pulled Shanaya towards him the moment they stepped into their home.

"Better believe it. It is true." With those words, Shanaya kissed his forehead to prove it.

Moving a little, he responded, "Agree with you completely." He swooped down to claim her lips and sealed their deal of love.

"Now if you don't move, we are going to be late for the book launch, and the author should not be late, right?" demanded Shanaya.

Sid laughed in agreement. Her eyes sparkled with love for him. She knew that life had thrown hardships at them, but they had fought together with love, and she was sure that they would continue to do so in the future.

It was time for a new beginning. Their time had come!

******THE BEGINNING******